LIFE AND ART

*The hitherto unpublished photograph
of Thomas Hardy on the title page is
by Bernard Griffin, Dorchester, England*

LIFE AND ART BY
THOMAS HARDY
ESSAYS NOTES AND
LETTERS COLLECTED
FOR THE FIRST TIME
WITH INTRODUCTION BY
ERNEST BRENNECKE JR
GREENBERG PUBLISHER
NEW YORK MCMXXV

HASKELL HOUSE
Publishers of Scholarly Books
NEW YORK
1966

First Published 1925

HASKELL HOUSE PUBLISHERS LTD.
Publishers of Scarce Scholarly Books
280 LAFAYETTE STREET
NEW YORK, N. Y. 10012

Library of Congress Catalog Card Number: 68-751

Standard Book Number 8383-0650-0

Printed in the United States of America

Contents

[vii]

Contents

FRONTISPIECE

FACSIMILE—AUTOGRAPH: 'WHY I DON'T WRITE
PLAYS' (From the *Pall Mall Budget*, 1st September, 1892).

The
INTRODUCTION

IN this book are assembled the more important reminiscential and critical writings which Thomas Hardy has had printed at various times. The first of these he wrote as long ago as 1865, six years before the appearance of his earliest novel; the last in 1923. In length, they range from brief epistolary paragraphs to extended and carefully worked out essays; in scope, they cover personal reactions to problems of philosophy, art and literature. Heretofore they have been available only in quaint, dusty back-numbers of newspapers and periodicals, tragically yellowing and crumbling on library shelves. They have not yet won a place in any of the several 'definitive' editions of the complete Hardy, and perhaps they never will.

This omission is possibly very just. Hardy's opinions do not belong with his imaginative works. They stand apart, an interesting miniature unit, magnificently overshadowed by his fiction and poetry.

And yet, by very reason of the magnificence of Hardy's major achievements, these little pieces are endowed not only with a fascination for his admirers, but also with a very definite importance for his more scientific critics. /

[1]

Life and Art

The personality of this author has long been enveloped in what has been complainingly called his 'inaccessibility.' He leads, indeed, a retired life, in the quiet Dorsetshire country, in a house set in dense foliage, invisible from the roadway. He refuses autographs and objects to interviewers. He 'cannot understand,' he once told me, people who are forever dashing about and hanging around, like St. Paul's Greeks, seeking some new thing. This is not strange. He has nearly completed his eighty-fifth year.

It is also, in a large measure, justified. Those who want to know Hardy as he wants to be known and as he undoubtedly will be known for many generations to come have only to buy and read his books, preferably his poetry, which he has called the more individual part of his output. At the same time, he has again and again requested his audiences not to identify the author with the creatures of his invention, nor his lucubrations with their emotions and opinions. This applies particularly to his novels, which, from *Desperate Remedies* to *Jude,* have by many been taken erroneously as autobiography, and to his lyric poetry, which he wishes to be considered dramatic even when not patently so.

Thus Hardy recognizes a distinct, if not unbridgeable, cleft between his works and his life, between the spirit of the poet and the personality of the man. In the act of creation, he has declared, some natures find themselves vocal to comedy, some to tragedy; and his own creative mood has responded predominantly to the tragic aspects of life. This must not be taken, however, as tantamount to a declaration that he does not realize the existence of other and totally different aspects. He has

The Introduction

lived in one world, and created another. This latter I
have elsewhere termed 'Thomas Hardy's Universe,' and
have shown its affinities with the system of idealistic
monism previously exposed by Schopenhauer. It is by
far the more important of the two worlds; it will last
longer than any of us; it may become immortal.

It matters little that we cannot positively identify
the *W.H.* to whom Shakespeare dedicated his sonnets; it
does matter tremendously that we have *Hamlet* and
Lear. The *Odyssey* matters, but not Homer's birth-
place. And it does not matter if we shall never know
just what Hardy thinks of Shaw or Wells, so long as we
have *The Dynasts*. Hardy himself has realized this, and
has let it go at that.

The cleavage I am indicating here is too frequently
forgotten. Its recognition often distinguishes an artist
of genius like Hardy from one of talent like George
Moore; it more often distinguishes a just critic from an
unjust or impertinent one.

If we can carry this firmly in mind, we shall be in a
fairer, if humbler, position in permitting ourselves the
antipodean realization, of a distinctly lower order of importance, that there must still be some sort of necessitated or causal interaction between the external or actual
Hardy-mentality, formed by physical events, and the
imaginative world in which he has presented his readers
opportunities to lead many vicarious existences.

It is natural that the curious should occasionally feel
the wish to 'get under the skin' of their favorite author,
to know both the kind of shoes he wears and the kind of
thoughts he indulges. Of this side of Hardy, which certainly has its points of interest (heightened indeed by

Life and Art

the colossal stature of the subject), the more significant
aspects are in this volume made accessible.

We find in the following pages the Hardy who speaks
for himself, familiarly and fearlessly. While in his
'poetic,' every opinion expressed or implied must be discounted as drama, here in his 'rhetoric' nothing need
be discounted as having been inserted for its imaginative effect. These outspoken reactions to life and its expression represent deliberate, considered self-exposures
of the man; they are in the nature of autobiography,
one or two of them actually published as such.

The three essays on the art of fiction, written and published when Hardy was at the height of his powers as a
novelist, will naturally claim the greatest attention.
They are as pertinent to the present-day problems of
the good and the bad, the decent and the indecent, in
realistic technique, as they were when they were composed. Here in his æsthetic, the author is observed to
gather his most powerful ammunition from the best
classical precedents and to discharge it at the modern
situation with uncanny marksmanship.

'A philosophy which appears between the inverted
commas of a dialogue may, with propriety, be as full
of holes as a sieve, if the person or persons who advance it gain any reality of humanity thereby . . .

'The novels which most conduce to moral uplift are
likely to be among those written without a moral purpose . . .

'A novel which does moral injury to a dozen imbeciles,
and has bracing results upon a thousand intellects of
normal vigor, can justify its existence, and probably a
novel was never written by the purest-minded author for

The Introduction

which there could not be found some moral invalid or other whom it was capable of harming . . .

'The crash of broken commandments is as necessary an accompaniment to the catastrophe of a tragedy as is the noise of a drum and cymbals to a triumphal march. But the crash of broken commandments shall not be heard; or, if at all, but gently, like the roaring of Bottom—gently as any sucking dove, or as 'twere any nightingale, lest we should fright the ladies out of their wits . . .

'Once in a crowd a listener heard a needy and illiterate woman saying of another poor and haggard woman who had lost her little son years before: "You can see the ghost of that child in her face even now."

'That speaker was one who, though she could probably neither read nor write, had the true means towards the "science" of fiction innate within her; a power of observation informed by a living heart . . .'

When Hardy delivers himself of trenchancies of this order of penetration, one almost begins to regret that he never saw fit to don the shining armor of criticism and prance bravely out into the lists in defense of literary courage and beauty. But undoubtedly he rightly felt that example would be more effective than precept. His *Tess* has attained even cinema-popularity, but only bibliographers can locate off-hand his *Candour in English Fiction*.

It is therefore all the more refreshing to listen to Hardy when he passes gentle unpleasantries on the character of gallant M. Maeterlinck's Lady Nature, and to witness his generous salute to M. Anatole France.

Of more particular personal interest are the notes on

Life and Art

subjects which have become peculiarly identified with the Wessex novels and poems: the dialect of the country, a more direct descendant of King Alfred's speech than our London English; the priceless Dorset peasantry; the unique and benevolent figure of the Reverend William Barnes.

Satisfying biographical items are the early letter to 'old Tinsley' the publisher, revealing the arrangements under which *Desperate Remedies* achieved, after a struggle, the perhaps undeserved dignity of print, and in contrast, the late letter to the Stevenson Club, declining the honorary membership offered when the struggle for recognition had been decisively won and when the needy seeker had become the shy sought.

The quasi-autobiography of Hardy's first printed piece, *How I Built Myself a House,* demonstrates by its feebleness the lateness of the flowering of the prose-writer's genius; it makes pleasant reading, but gives little indication of the powers latent in its author's pen. It is interesting here chiefly because it dates from the same period as that covered in the genuinely autobiographical *Memories of Church Restoration,* which succeeded it after an eventful interval of forty-one years.

There would be little excuse for publishing such an apparently heterogeneous collection as this during Hardy's lifetime, if one were not firmly convinced that it possessed both extrinsic, permanent value as a revelation of the personality of the greatest poet of his day, and intrinsic interest in its quality of forceful expression of keen sensibility and excellent sense.

E. B.

NEW YORK, *September,* 1924.

The Essays

How I Built Myself a House

Hardy's first published piece. First appeared in *Chambers's Journal of Popular Literature, Science and Arts*, March 18, 1865.

MY wife Sophia, myself, and the beginning of a happy line, formerly lived in the suburbs of London, in the sort of house called a Highly-Desirable Semi-detached Villa. But in reality our residence was the very opposite of what we wished it to be. We had no room for our friends when they visited us, and we were obliged to keep our coal out of doors in a heap against the back-wall. If we managed to squeeze a few acquaintances round our table to dinner, there was very great difficulty in serving it; and on such occasions the maid, for want of sideboard room, would take to putting the dishes in the staircase, or on stools and chairs in the passage, so that if anybody else came after we had sat down, he usually went away again, disgusted at seeing the remains of what we had already got through standing in these places, and perhaps the celery waiting in a corner hard by. It was therefore only natural that on wet days, chimney-sweepings, and those cleaning times when chairs may be seen with their legs upwards, a tub blocking a doorway, and yourself walking about edgeways among the things, we called the villa hard names, and that we resolved to escape from it as soon as it would be politic, in a monetary sense, to carry out a notion which had long been in our minds.

[9]

Life and Art

This notion was to build a house of our own a little further out of town than where we had hitherto lived. The new residence was to be right and proper in every respect. It was to be of some mysterious size and proportion, which would make us both peculiarly happy ever afterwards—that had always been a settled thing. It was neither to cost too much nor too little, but just enough to fitly inaugurate the new happiness. Its situation was to be in a healthy spot, on a stratum of dry gravel, about ninety feet above the springs. There were to be trees to the north, and a pretty view to the south. It was also to be easily accessible by rail.

Eighteen months ago, a third baby being our latest blessing, we began to put the above-mentioned ideas into practice. As the house itself, rather than its position, is what I wish particularly to speak of, I will not dwell upon the innumerable difficulties that were to be overcome before a suitable spot could be found. Maps marked out in little pink and green oblongs clinging to a winding road became as familiar to my eyes as my own hand. I learned, too, all about the coloured plans of Land to be Let for Building Purposes, which are exhibited at railway stations and in agents' windows—that sketches of cabbages in rows, or artistically irregular, meant large trees that would afford a cooling shade when they had been planted and had grown up—that patches of blue shewed fishponds and fountains; and that a wide straight road to the edge of the map was the way to the station, a corner of which was occasionally shewn, as if it would come within a convenient distance, disguise the fact as the owners might.

After a considerable time had been spent in these

How I Built Myself a House

studies, I began to see that some of our intentions in the matter of site must be given up. The trees to the north went first. After a short struggle, they were followed by the ninety feet above the springs. Sophia, with all wifely tenacity, stuck to the pretty view long after I was beaten about the gravel subsoil. In the end, we decided upon a place imagined to be rather convenient, and rather healthy, but possessing no other advantage worth mentioning. I took it on a lease for the established period, ninety-nine years.

We next thought about an architect. A friend of mine, who sometimes sends a paper on art and science to the magazines, strongly recommended Mr. Penny, a gentleman whom he considered to have architectural talent of every kind, but if he was a trifle more skilful in any one branch of his profession than in another, it was in designing excellent houses for families of moderate means. I at once proposed to Sophia that we should think over some arrangement of rooms which would be likely to suit us, and then call upon the architect, that he might put our plan into proper shape.

I made my sketch, and my wife made hers. Her drawing and dining rooms were very large, nearly twice the size of mine, though her doors and windows shewed sound judgment. We soon found that there was no such thing as fitting our ideas together, do what we would. When we had come to no conclusion at all, we called at Mr. Penny's office. I began telling him my business, upon which he took a sheet of foolscap, and made numerous imposing notes, with large brackets and dashes to them. Sitting there with him in his office, surrounded by rolls of paper, circles, squares, triangles, compasses, and many other of the inventions which have been sought out by men from time to time, and perceiving that all these were the realities which had been faintly shadowed forth to me by Euclid some years before, it is no wonder that I became a puppet in his hands. He settled everything in a miraculous way. We were told the only possible size we could have the rooms, the only way we should be allowed to go upstairs, and the exact quantity of wine we might order at once, so as to fit the wine cellar he had in his head. His professional opinions, propelled by his facts, seemed to float into my mind whether I wished to receive them or not. I thought at the time that Sophia, from her silence, was in the same helpless state; but she has since told me it was quite otherwise, and that she was only a little tired.

I had been very anxious all along that the stipulated cost, eighteen hundred pounds, should not be exceeded, and I impressed this again upon Mr. Penny.

'I will give you an approximate estimate for the sort of thing we are thinking of,' he said. 'Linem.' (This was the clerk.)

'Did you speak, sir?'

'Forty-nine by fifty-four by twenty-eight, twice fourteen by thirty-one by eleven, and several small items which we will call one hundred and sixty.'

'Eighty-two thousand four hundred'——

'But eighteen hundred at the very outside,' I began, 'is what'——

'Feet, my dear sir—feet, cubic feet,' said Mr. Penny. 'Put it down at sixpence a foot, Linem, remainders not an object.'

How I Built Myself a House

'Two thousand two hundred pounds.' This was too much.

'Well, try it at something less, leaving out all below hundreds, Linem.'

'About eighteen hundred and seventy pounds.'

'Very satisfactory, in my opinion,' said Mr. Penny, turning to me. 'What do you think?'

'You are so particular, John,' interrupted my wife. 'I am sure it is exceedingly moderate: elegance and extreme cheapness never do go together.'

(It may be here remarked that Sophia never calls me 'my dear' before strangers. She considers that, like the ancient practice in besieged cities of throwing loaves over the walls, it really denotes a want rather than an abundance of them within.)

I did not trouble the architect any further, and we rose to leave.

'Be sure you make a nice conservatory, Mr. Penny,' said my wife; 'something that has character about it. If it could only be in the Chinese style, with beautiful ornaments at the corners, like Mrs. Smith's, only better,' she continued, turning to me with a glance in which a broken tenth commandment might have been seen.

'Some sketches shall be forwarded, which I think will suit you,' answered Mr. Penny pleasantly, looking as if he had possessed for some years a complete guide to the minds of all people who intended to build.

It is needless to go through the whole history of the plan-making. A builder had been chosen, and the house marked out, when we went down to the place one morning to see how the foundations looked.

Life and Art

It is a strange fact, that a person's new house drawn in outline on the ground where it is to stands, looks ridiculously and inconveniently small. The notion it gives one is, that any portion of one's after-life spent within such boundaries must of necessity be rendered wretched on account of bruises daily received by running against the partitions, doorposts, and fireplaces. In my case, the lines shewing sitting-rooms seemed to denote cells; the kitchen looked as if it might develop into a large box; whilst the study appeared to consist chiefly of a fireplace and a door. We were told that houses always looked so; but Sophia's disgust at the sight of such a diminutive drawing-room was not to be lessened by any scientific reasoning. Six feet longer—four feet then—three it must be, she argued; and the room was accordingly lengthened. I felt rather relieved when at last I got her off the ground and on the road home.

The building gradually crept upwards, and put forth chimneys. We were standing beside it one day, looking at the men at work on the top, when the builders' foreman came towards us.

'Being your own house, sir, and as we are finishing the last chimney, you would perhaps like to go up,' he said.

'I am sure I should much, if I were a man,' was my wife's observation to me. 'The landscape must appear so lovely from that height.'

This remark placed me in something of a dilemma, for it must be confessed that I am not given to climbing. The sight of cliffs, roofs, scaffoldings, and elevated places in general, which have no sides to keep people from slipping off, always causes me to feel how infinitely

How I Built Myself a House

preferable a position at the bottom is to a position at the top of them. But as my house was by no means lofty, and it was but for once, I said I would go up.

My knees felt a good deal in the way as I ascended the ladder; but that was not so disagreeable as the thrill which passed through me as I followed my guide along two narrow planks, one bending beneath each foot. However, having once started, I kept on, and next climbed another ladder, thin and weak-looking, and not tied at the top. I could not help thinking, as I viewed the horizon between the steps, what a shocking thing it would be if any part should break; and to get rid of the thought, I adopted the device of mentally criticising the leading articles in that morning's *Times;* but as the plan did not answer, I tried to fancy that, though strangely enough it seemed otherwise, I was only four feet from the ground. This was a failure too; and just as I had commenced upon an idea that great quantities of featherbeds were spread below, I reached the top scaffold.

'Rather high,' I said to the foreman, trying, but failing, to appear unconcerned.

'Well, no,' he answered; 'nothing to what it is sometimes (I'll just trouble you not to step upon the end of that plank there, as it will turn over); though you may as well fall from here as from the top of the Monument for the matter of life being quite extinct when they pick you up,' he continued, looking around at the weather and the crops, as it were.

Then a workingman, with a load of bricks, stamped along the boards, and overturned them at my feet, causing me to shake up and down like the little servant-men behind private cabs. I asked, in trepidation, if the bricks

Life and Art

were not dangerously heavy, thinking of a newspaper paragraph headed 'Frightful Accident from an Overloaded Scaffold.'

'Just what I was going to say. Dan has certainly too many there,' answered the man. 'But it won't break down if we walk without springing, and don't sneeze, though the mortar-boy's whooping-cough was strong enough in my poor brother Jim's case,' he continued abstractedly, as if he himself possessed several necks, and could afford to break one or two.

My wife was picking daisies a little distance off, apparently in a state of complete indifference as to whether I was on the scaffold, at the foot of it, or in St. George's Hospital; so I roused myself for a descent, and tried the small ladder. I cannot accurately say how I did get down; but during that performance, my body seemed perforated by holes, through which breezes blew in all directions. As I got nearer the earth, they went away. It may be supposed that my wife's notion of the height differed considerably from my own, and she inquired particularly for the landscape, which I had quite forgotten; but the discovery of that fact did not cause me to break a resolution not to trouble my chimneys again.

Beyond a continual anxiety and frequent journeyings along the sides of a triangle, of which the old house, the new house, and the architect's office were the corners, nothing worth mentioning happened till the building was nearly finished. Sophia's ardour in the business, which at the beginning was so intense, had nearly burned itself out, so I was left pretty much to myself in getting over the later difficulties. Amongst them was the question of a porch. I had often been annoyed whilst waiting out-

How I Built Myself a House

side a door on a wet day at being exposed to the wind and rain, and it was my favourite notion that I would have a model porch whenever I should build a house. Thus it was very vexing to recollect, just as the workmen were finishing it off, that I had never mentioned the subject to Mr. Penny, and that he had not suggested anything about one to me.

'A porch or no porch is entirely a matter of personal feeling and taste,' was his remark, in answer to a complaint from me; 'so, of course, I did not put one without its being mentioned. But it happens that in this case it would be an improvement—a feature, in fact. There is this objection, that the roof will close up the window of the little place on the landing; but we may get ventilation by making an opening higher up, if you don't mind a trifling darkness, or rather gloom.'

My first thought was that this might tend to reduce myself and family to a state of chronic melancholy; but remembering there were reflectors advertised to throw sunlight into any nook almost, I agreed to the inconvenience, for the sake of the porch, though I found afterwards that the gloom was for all time, the patent reflector, naturally enough, sending its spot of light against the opposite wall, where it was not wanted, and leaving none about the landing, where it was.

In getting a house built for a specified sum by contract with a builder, there is a certain pit-fall into which unwary people are sure to step—this accident is technically termed 'getting into extras.' It is evident that the only way to get out again without making a town-talk about yourself is to pay the builder a large sum of money over and above the contract amount—the value of course of

Life and Art

the extras. In the present case, I knew very well that the perceptible additions would have to be paid for. Common sense, and Mr. Penny himself perhaps, should have told me a little more distinctly that I must pay if I said 'yes' to questions whether I preferred one window a trifle larger than it was originally intended, another a trifle smaller, second thoughts as to where a doorway should be, and so on. Then came a host of things 'not included' —a sink in the scullery, a rain-water tank and a pump, a trap-door into the room, a scraper, a weather-cock and four letters, ventilators in the nursery, same in the kitchen, all of which worked vigorously enough, but the wrong way; patent remarkable bell-pulls; a royal letters extraordinary kitchen-range, which it would cost exactly threepence three-farthings to keep a fire in for twelve hours, and yet cook any joint in any way, warm up what was left yesterday, boil the vegetables, and do the ironing. But not keeping a strict account of all these expenses, and thinking myself safe in Mr. Penny's hands from any enormous increase, I was astounded to find that the additions altogether came to some hundreds of pounds. I could almost go through the worry of building another house, to shew how carefully I would avoid getting into extras again.

Then they have to be wound up. A surveyor is called in from somewhere, and, by a fiction, his heart's desire is supposed to be that you shall not be overcharged one halfpenny by the builder for the additions. The builder names a certain sum as the value of a portion—say double its worth, the surveyor then names a sum, about half its true value. They then fight it out by word of mouth, and gradually bringing their valuations nearer and

[18]

How I Built Myself a House

nearer together, at last meet in the middle. All my accounts underwent this operation.

A Families-removing van carried our furniture and effects to the new building without giving us much trouble; but a number of vexing little incidents occurred on our settling down, which I should have felt more deeply had not a sort of Martinmas summer of Sophia's interest in the affair now set in, and lightened them considerably. Smoke was one of our nuisances. On lighting the study-fire, every particle of smoke came curling into the room. In our trouble, we sent for the architect, who immediately asked if we had tried the plan of opening the register to cure it. We had not, but we did so, and the smoke ascended at once. The last thing I remember was Sophia jumping up one night and frightening me out of my senses with the exclamation: 'O that builder! Not a single bar of any sort is there to the nursery-windows. John, some day those poor little children will tumble out in their innocence—how should they know better?—and be dashed to pieces. Why *did* you put the nursery on the second floor?' And you may be sure that some bars were put up the very next morning.

The Dorsetshire Labourer

First appeared in *Longman's Magazine*, July, 1883.

I T seldom happens that a nickname which affects to portray a class is honestly indicative of the individuals composing that class. The few features distinguishing them from other bodies of men have been seized on and exaggerated, while the incomparably more numerous features common to all humanity have been ignored. In the great world this wild colouring of so-called typical portraits is clearly enough recognised. Nationalities, the aristocracy, the plutocracy, the citizen class, and many others have their allegorical representatives, which are received with due allowance for flights of imagination in the direction of burlesque.

But when the class lies somewhat out of the ken of ordinary society the caricature begins to be taken as truth. Moreover, the original is held to be an actual unit of the multitude signified. He ceases to be an abstract figure and becomes a sample. Thus when we arrive at the farm-labouring community we find it to be seriously personified by the pitiable picture known as Hodge; not only so, but the community is assumed to be a uniform collection of concrete Hodges.

This supposed real but highly conventional Hodge is a degraded being of uncouth manner and aspect, stolid understanding, and snail-like movement. His speech is such a chaotic corruption of regular language that few persons of progressive aims consider it worth while to enquire what views, if any, of life, of nature, or of so-

[20]

The Dorsetshire Labourer

ciety, are conveyed in these utterances. Hodge hangs his head or looks sheepish when spoken to, and thinks Lunnon a place paved with gold. Misery and fever lurk in his cottage, while, to paraphrase the words of a recent writer on the labouring classes, in his future there are only the workhouse and the grave. He hardly dares to think at all. He has few thoughts of joy, and little hope of rest. His life slopes into a darkness not 'quieted by hope.'

If one of the many thoughtful persons who hold this view were to go by rail to Dorset, where Hodge in his most unmitigated form is supposed to reside, and seek out a retired district, he might by and by certainly meet a man who, at first contact with an intelligence fresh from the contrasting world of London, would seem to exhibit some of the above-mentioned qualities. The latter items in the list, the mental miseries, the visitor might hardly look for in their fulness, since it would have become perceptible to him as an explorer, and to any but the chamber theorist, that no uneducated community, rich or poor, bond or free, possessing average health and personal liberty, could exist in an unchangeable slough of despond, or that it would for many months if it could. Its members, like the accursed swine, would rush down a steep place and be choked in the waters. He would have learnt that wherever a mode of supporting life is neither noxious nor absolutely inadequate, there springs up happiness, and will spring up happiness, of some sort or other. Indeed, it is among such communities as these that happiness will find her last refuge on earth, since it is among them that a perfect insight into the conditions of existence will be longest postponed.

Life and Art

That in their future there are only the workhouse and the grave is no more and no less true than that in the future of the average well-to-do householder there are only the invalid chair and the brick vault.

Waiving these points, however, the investigator would insist that the man he had encountered exhibited a suspicious blankness of gaze, a great uncouthness and inactivity; and he might truly approach the unintelligible if addressed by a stranger on any but the commonest subject. But suppose that, by some accident, the visitor were obliged to go home with this man, take pot-luck with him and his, as one of the family. For the nonce the very sitting down would seem an undignified performance, and at first, the ideas, the modes, and the surroundings generally, would be puzzling—even impenetrable; or if in a measure penetrable, would seem to have but little meaning. But living on there for a few days the sojourner would become conscious of a new aspect in the life around him. He would find that, without any objective change whatever, variety had taken the place of monotony; that the man who had brought him home— the typical Hodge, as he conjectured—was somehow not typical of anyone but himself. His host's brothers, uncles, and neighbours, as they became personally known, would appear as different from his host himself as one member of a club, or inhabitant of a city street, from another. As, to the eye of a diver, contrasting colours shine out by degrees from what has originally painted itself of an unrelieved earthy hue, so would shine out the characters, capacities, and interests of these people to him. He would, for one thing, find that the lan-

The Dorsetshire Labourer

guage, instead of being a vile corruption of cultivated speech, was a tongue with a grammatical inflection rarely disregarded by his entertainer, though his entertainer's children would occasionally make a sad hash of their talk. Having attended the National School they would mix the printed tongue as taught therein with the unwritten, dying, Wessex English that they had learnt of their parents, the result of this transitional state of theirs being a composite language without rule or harmony.

Six months pass, and our gentleman leaves the cottage, bidding his friends good-bye with genuine regret. The great change in his perception is that Hodge, the dull, unvarying, joyless one, has ceased to exist for him. He has become disintegrated into a number of dissimilar fellow-creatures, men of many minds, infinite in difference; some happy, many serene, a few depressed; some clever, even to genius, some stupid, some wanton, some austere; some mutely Miltonic, some Cromwellian; into men who have private views of each other, as he has of his friends; who applaud or condemn each other; amuse or sadden themselves by the contemplation of each other's foibles or vices; and each of whom walks in his own way the road to dusty death. Dick the carter, Bob the shepherd, and Sam the ploughman, are, it is true, alike in the narrowness of their means and their general open-air life; but they cannot be rolled together again into such a Hodge as he dreamt of, by any possible enchantment. And should time and distance render an abstract being, representing the field labourer, possible again to the mind of the inquirer (a questionable possi-

Life and Art

bility) he will find that the Hodge of current conception no longer sums up the capacities of the class so defined.

The pleasures enjoyed by the Dorset labourer may be far from pleasures of the highest kind desirable for him. They may be pleasures of the wrong shade. And the inevitable glooms of a straitened hard-working life occasionally enwrap him from such pleasures as he has; and in times of special storm and stress the 'Complaint of Piers the Ploughman' is still echoed in his heart. But even Piers had his flights of merriment and humour; and ploughmen as a rule do not give sufficient thought to the morrow to be miserable when not in physical pain. Drudgery in the slums and alleys of a city, too long pursued, and accompanied as it too often is by indifferent health, may induce a mood of despondency which is well-nigh permanent; but the same degree of drudgery in the fields results at worst in a mood of painless passivity. A pure atmosphere and a pastoral environment are a very appreciable portion of the sustenance which tends to produce the sound mind and body, and thus much sustenance is, at least, the labourer's birthright.

If it were possible to gauge the average sufferings of classes, the probability is that in Dorsetshire the figure would be lower with the regular farmer's labourers— 'workfolk' as they call themselves—than with the adjoining class, the unattached labourers, approximating to the free labourers of the middle ages, who are to be found in the larger villages and small towns of the county—many of them, no doubt, descendants of the old copyholders who were ousted from their little plots when the system of leasing large farms grew general. They are, what the regular labourer is not, out of sight

The Dorsetshire Labourer

of patronage; and to be out of sight is to be out of mind when misfortune arises, and pride or sensitiveness leads them to conceal their privations.

The happiness of a class can rarely be estimated aright by philosophers who look down upon that class from the Olympian heights of society. Nothing, for instance, is more common than for some philanthropic lady to burst in upon a family, be struck by the apparent squalor of the scene, and to straightway mark down that household in her note-book as a frightful example of the misery of the labouring classes. There are two distinct probabilities of error in forming any such estimate. The first is that the apparent squalor is no squalor at all. I am credibly informed that the conclusion is nearly always based on *colour*. A cottage in which the walls, the furniture, and the dress of the inmates reflect the brighter rays of the solar spectrum is read by these amiable visitors as a cleanly, happy home while one whose prevailing hue happens to be dingy russet, or a quaint old leather tint, or any of the numerous varieties of mud colour, is thought necessarily the abode of filth and Giant Despair. 'I always kip a white apron behind the door to slip on when the gentlefolk knock, for if so be they see a white apron they think ye be clane,' said an honest woman one day, whose bedroom floors could have been scraped with as much advantage as a pigeon-loft; but who, by a judicious use of high lights, shone as a pattern of neatness in her patrons' eyes.

There was another woman who had long nourished an unreasoning passion for burnt umber, and at last acquired a pot of the same from a friendly young carpenter. With this pigment she covered every surface

Life and Art

in her residence to which paint is usually applied, and having more left, and feeling that to waste it would be a pity as times go, she went on to cover other surfaces till the whole was consumed. Her dress and that of the children were mostly of faded snuff-colour, her natural thrift inducing her to cut up and re-make a quantity of old stuffs that had been her mother's; and to add to the misery the floor of her cottage was of Mayne brick—a material which has the complexion of gravy mottled with cinders. Notwithstanding that the bed-linen and underclothes of this unfortunate woman's family were like the driven snow, and that the insides of her cooking utensils were concave mirrors, she was used with great effect as the frightful example of slovenliness for many years in that neighbourhood.

The second probability arises from the error of supposing that actual slovenliness is always accompanied by unhappiness. If it were so, a windfall of any kind would be utilised in most cases in improving the surroundings. But the money always goes in the acquisition of something new, and not in the removal of what there is already too much of, dirt. And most frequently the grimiest families are not the poorest; nay, paradoxical as it may seem, external neglect in a household implies something above the lowest level of poverty. Copyholders, cottage freeholders, and the like, are as a rule less trim and neat, more muddling in their ways, than the dependent labourer; and yet there is no more comfortable or serene being than the cottager who is sure of his roof. An instance of probable error through inability to see below the surface of things occurred the other day in an article by a lady on the peasant pro-

The Dorsetshire Labourer

prietors of Auvergne. She states that she discovered these persons living on an earth floor, mixed up with onions, dirty clothes, and the 'indescribable remnants of never stirred rubbish'; while one of the houses had no staircase, the owners of the premises reaching their bedrooms by climbing up a bank, and stepping in at the higher level. This was an inconvenient way of getting upstairs; but we must guard against the inference that because these peasant proprietors are in a slovenly condition, and certain English peasants who are not proprietors live in model cottages copied out of a book by the squire, the latter are so much happier than the former as the dignity of their architecture is greater. It were idle to deny that, other things being equal, the family which dwells in a cleanly and spacious cottage has the probability of a more cheerful existence than a family narrowly housed and draggletailed. It has guarantees for health which the other has not. But it must be remembered that melancholy among the rural poor arises primarily from a sense of the incertitude and precariousness of their position. Like Burns's field-mouse, they are overawed and timorous lest those who can wrong them should be inclined to exercise their power. When we know that the Damocles' sword of the poor is the fear of being turned out of their houses by the farmer or squire, we may wonder how many scrupulously clean English labourers would not be glad with half-an-acre of the complaint that afflicts these unhappy freeholders of Auvergne.

It is not at all uncommon to find among the workfolk philosophers who recognise, as clearly as Lord Palmerston did, that dirt is only matter in the wrong place. A

Life and Art

worthy man holding these wide views had put his clean shirt on a gooseberry bush one Sunday morning, to be aired in the sun, whence it blew off into the mud, and was much soiled. His wife would have got him another, but, 'No,' he said, 'the shirt shall wear his week. 'Tis fresh dirt, anyhow, and starch is no more.'

On the other hand, true poverty—that is, the actual want of necessaries—is constantly trying to be decent, and one of the clearest signs of deserving poverty is the effort it makes to appear otherwise by scrupulous neatness.

To see the Dorset labourer at his worst and saddest time, he should be viewed when attending a wet hiring-fair at Candlemas, in search of a new master. His natural cheerfulness bravely struggles against the weather and the incertitude; but as the day passes on, and his clothes get wet through, and he is still unhired, there does appear a factitiousness in the smile which, with a self-repressing mannerliness hardly to be found among any other class, he yet has ready when he encounters and talks with friends who have been more fortunate. In youth and manhood, this disappointment occurs but seldom; but at threescore and over, it is frequently the lot of those who have no sons and daughters to fall back upon, or whose children are ingrates, or far away.

Here, at the corner of the street, in this aforesaid wet hiring-fair, stands an old shepherd. He is evidently a lonely man. The battle of life has always been a sharp one with him, for, to begin with, he is a man of small frame. He is now so bowed by hard work and years that, approaching from behind, you can scarcely see his

The Dorsetshire Labourer

head. He has planted the stem of his crook in the gutter, and rests upon the bow, which is polished to silver brightness by the long friction of his hands. He has quite forgotten where he is and what he has come for, his eyes being bent on the ground. 'There's work in en,' says one farmer to another, as they look dubiously across; 'there's work left in en still; but not so much as I want for my acreage.' 'You'd get en cheap,' says the other. The shepherd does not hear them, and there seem to be passing through his mind pleasant visions of the hiring successes of his prime—when his skill in ovine surgery laid open any farm to him for the asking, and his employer would say uneasily in the early days of February, 'You don't mean to leave us this year?'

But the hale and strong have not to wait thus, and having secured places in the morning, the day passes merrily enough with them.

The hiring-fair of recent years presents an appearance unlike that of former times. A glance up the high street of the town on a Candlemas-fair day twenty or thirty years ago revealed a crowd whose general colour was whity-brown flecked with white. Black was almost absent, the few farmers who wore that shade being hardly discernible. Now the crowd is as dark as a London crowd. This change is owing to the rage for cloth clothes which possesses the labourers of to-day. Formerly they came in smock-frocks and gaiters, the shepherds with their crooks, the carters with a zone of whipcord round their hats, thatchers with a straw tucked into the brim, and so on. Now, with the exception of the crook in the hands of an occasional old shepherd, there is no mark of speciality in the groups, who might be

Life and Art

tailors or undertakers' men, for what they exhibit externally. Out of a group of eight, for example, who talk together in the middle of the road, only one wears corduroy trousers. Two wear cloth pilot-coats and black trousers, two patterned tweed suits with black canvas overalls, the remaining four suits being of faded broadcloth. To a great extent these are their Sunday suits; but the genuine white smock-frock of Russia duck and the whity-brown one of drabbet, are rarely seen now afield, except on the shoulders of old men. Where smocks are worn by the young and middle-aged, they are of blue material. The mechanic's 'slop' has also been adopted; but a mangy old cloth coat is preferred; so that often a group of these honest fellows on the arable has the aspect of a body of tramps up to some mischief in the field, rather than its natural tillers at work there.

That peculiarity of the English urban poor (which M. Taine ridicules, and unfavourably contrasts with the taste of the Continental working-people)—their preference for the cast-off clothes of a richer class to a special attire of their own—has, in fact, reached the Dorset farm folk. Like the men, the women are, pictorially, less interesting than they used to be. Instead of the wing bonnet like the tilt of a waggon, cotton gown, bright-hued neckerchief, and strong flat boots and shoes, they (the younger ones at least) wear shabby millinery bonnets and hats with beads and feathers, 'material' dresses, and boot-heels almost as foolishly shaped as those of ladies of highest education.

Having 'agreed for a place,' as it is called, either at the fair, or (occasionally) by private intelligence, or

The Dorsetshire Labourer

(with growing frequency) by advertisement in the penny local papers, the terms are usually reduced to writing: though formerly a written agreement was unknown, and is now, as a rule, avoided by the farmer if the labourer does not insist upon one. It is signed by both, and a shilling is passed to bind the bargain. The business is then settled, and the man returns to his place of work, to do no more in the matter till Lady Day, Old Style—April 6.

Of all the days in the year, people who love the rural poor of the south-west should pray for a fine day then. Dwellers near the highways of the country are reminded of the anniversary surely enough. They are conscious of a disturbance of their night's rest by noises beginning in the small hours of darkness, and intermittently continuing till daylight—noises as certain to recur on that particular night of the month as the voice of the cuckoo on the third or fourth week of the same. The day of fulfilment has come, and the labourers are on the point of being fetched from the old farm by the carters of the new. For it is always by the waggon and horses of the farmer who requires his services that the hired man is conveyed to his destination; and that this may be accomplished within the day is the reason that the noises begin so soon after midnight. Suppose the distance to be an ordinary one of a dozen or fifteen miles. The carter at the prospective place rises 'when Charles's Wain is over the new chimney,' harnesses his team of three horses by lantern light, and proceeds to the present home of his coming comrade. It is the passing of these empty waggons in all directions that is heard breaking the stillness of the hours before dawn. The aim is

usually to be at the door of the removing household by
six o'clock, when the loading of goods at once begins;
and at nine or ten the start to the new home is made.
From this hour till one or two in the day, when the other
family arrives at the old house, the cottage is empty, and
it is only in that short interval that the interior can be
in anyway cleaned and lime-whitened for the new
comers, however dirty it may have become, or whatever
sickness may have prevailed among members of the de-
parted family.

Should the migrant himself be a carter there is a slight
modification in the arrangement, for carters do not fetch
carters, as they fetch shepherds and general hands. In
this case the man has to transfer himself. He relin-
quishes charge of the horses of the old farm in the afternoon of April 5, and starts on foot the same afternoon
for the new place. There he makes the acquaintance of
the horses which are to be under his care for the ensuing
year, and passes the night sometimes on a bundle of
clean straw in the stable, for he is as yet a stranger
here, and too indifferent to the comforts of a bed on
this particular evening to take much trouble to secure
one. From this couch he uncurls himself about two
o'clock, a.m. (for the distance we have assumed), and,
harnessing his new charges, moves off with them to his
old home, where, on his arrival, the packing is already
advanced by the wife, and loading goes on as before
mentioned.

The goods are built up on the waggon to a well-nigh
unvarying pattern, which is probably as peculiar to the
country labourer as the hexagon to the bee. The dresser,
with its finger-marks and domestic evidences thick upon

The Dorsetshire Labourer

it, stands importantly in front, over the backs of the shaft horses, in its erect and natural position, like some Ark of the Covenant, which must not be handled slightingly or overturned. The hive of bees is slung up to the axle of the waggon, and alongside it the cooking pot or crock, within which are stowed the roots of garden flowers. Barrels are largely used for crockery, and budding gooseberry bushes are suspended by the roots; while on the top of the furniture a circular nest is made of the bed and bedding for the matron and children, who sit there through the journey. If there is no infant in arms, the woman holds the head of the clock, which at any exceptional lurch of the waggon strikes one, in thin tones. The other object of solicitude is the looking-glass, usually held in the lap of the eldest girl. It is emphatically spoken of as *the* looking-glass, there being but one in the house, except possibly a small shaving-glass for the husband. But labouring men are not much dependent upon mirrors for a clean chin. I have seen many men shaving in the chimney corner, looking into the fire; or, in summer, in the garden, with their eyes fixed upon a gooseberry-bush, gazing as steadfastly as if there were a perfect reflection of their image—from which it would seem that the concentrated look of shavers in general was originally demanded rather by the mind than by the eye. On the other hand, I knew a man who used to walk about the room all the time he was engaged in the operation, and how he escaped cutting himself was a marvel. Certain luxurious dandies of the furrow, who could not do without a reflected image of themselves when using the razor, obtained it till quite recently by placing the crown of an old hat outside the window-

Life and Art

pane, then confronting it inside the room and falling to
—a contrivance which formed a very clear reflection of
a face in high light.

The day of removal, if fine, wears an aspect of jollity,
and the whole proceeding is a blithe one. A bundle of
provisions for the journey is usually hung up at the side
of the vehicle, together with a three-pint stone jar of
extra strong ale; for it is as impossible to move house
without beer as without horses. Roadside inns, too, are
patronised, where, during the halt, a mug is seen ascend-
ing and descending through the air to and from the
feminine portion of the household at the top of the
waggon. The drinking at these times is, however, moderate, the beer supplied to travelling labourers being of
a preternaturally small brew; as was illustrated by a
dialogue which took place on such an occasion quite recently. The liquor was not quite to the taste of the
male travellers, and they complained. But the landlady
upheld its merits. ' 'Tis our own brewing, and there is
nothing in it but malt and hops,' she said, with recti-
tude. 'Yes, there is,' said the traveller. 'There's
water.' 'Oh! I forgot the water,' the landlady replied.
'I'm d——d if you did, mis'ess,' replied the man; 'for
there's hardly anything else in the cup.'

Ten or a dozen of these families, with their goods,
may be seen halting simultaneously at an out-of-the-way
inn, and it is not possible to walk a mile on any of the
high roads this day without meeting several. This annual migration from farm to farm is much in excess of
what it was formerly. For example, on a particular
farm where, a generation ago, not more than one cottage on an average changed occupants yearly, and where

[34]

The Dorsetshire Labourer

the majority remained all their lifetime, the whole number of tenants were changed at Lady Day just past, and this though nearly all of them had been new arrivals on the previous Lady Day. Dorset labourers now look upon an annual removal as the most natural thing in the world, and it becomes with the younger families a pleasant excitement. Change is also a certain sort of education. Many advantages accrue to the labourers from the varied experience it brings, apart from the discovery of the best market for their abilities. They have become shrewder and sharper men of the world, and have learnt how to hold their own with firmness and judgment. Whenever the habitually-removing man comes into contact with one of the old-fashioned stationary sort, who are still to be found, it is impossible not to perceive that the former is much more wide awake than his fellow-worker, astonishing him with stories of the wide world comprised in a twenty-mile radius from their homes.

They are also losing their peculiarities as a class; hence the humorous simplicity which formerly characterised the men and the unsophisticated modesty of the women are rapidly disappearing or lessening, under the constant attrition of lives mildly approximating to those of workers in a manufacturing town. It is the common remark of villagers immediately above the labouring class, who know the latter well as personal acquaintances, that 'there are no nice homely workfolk now as there used to be.' There may be, and is, some exaggeration in this, but it is only natural that, now different districts of them are shaken together once a year and redistributed, like a shuffled pack of cards, they have

Life and Art

ceased to be so local in feeling or manner as formerly, and have entered on the condition of inter-social citizens, 'whose city stretches the whole county over. Their brains are less frequently than they once were 'as dry as the remainder biscuit after a voyage,' and they vent less often the result of their own observations than what they have heard to be the current ideas of smart chaps in towns. The women have, in many districts, acquired the rollicking air of factory hands. That seclusion and immutability, which was so bad for their pockets, was an unrivalled fosterer of their personal charm in the eyes of those whose experiences had been less limited. But the artistic merit of their old condition is scarcely a reason why they should have continued in it when other communities were marching on so vigorously towards uniformity and mental equality. It is only the old story that progress and picturesqueness do not harmonise. They are losing their individuality, but they are widening the range of their ideas, and gaining in freedom. It is too much to expect them to remain stagnant and old-fashioned for the pleasure of romantic spectators.

But, picturesqueness apart, a result of this increasing nomadic habit of the labourer is naturally a less intimate and kindly relation with the land he tills than existed before enlightenment enabled him to rise above the condition of a serf who lived and died on a particular plot, like a tree. During the centuries of serfdom, of copyholding tenants, and down to twenty or thirty years ago, before the power of unlimited migration had been clearly realised, the husbandman of either class had the interest of long personal association with

[36]

The Dorsetshire Labourer

his farm. The fields were those he had ploughed and sown from boyhood, and it was impossible for him, in such circumstances, to sink altogether the character of natural guardian in that of hireling. Not so very many years ago, the landowner, if he were good for anything, stood as a court of final appeal in cases of the harsh dismissal of a man by the farmer. 'I'll go to my lord' was a threat which overbearing farmers respected, for 'my lord' had often personally known the labourer long before he knew the labourer's master. But such arbitrament is rarely practicable now. The landlord does not know by sight, if even by name, half the men who preserve his acres from the curse of Eden. They come and go yearly, like birds of passage, nobody thinks whence or whither. This dissociation is favoured by the customary system of letting the cottages with the land, so that, far from having a guarantee of a holding to keep him fixed, the labourer has not even the stability of a landlord's tenant; he is only tenant of a tenant, the latter possibly a new comer, who takes strictly commercial views of his man and cannot afford to waste a penny on sentimental considerations.

Thus, while their pecuniary condition in the prime of life is bettered, and their freedom enlarged, they have lost touch with their environment, and that sense of long local participancy which is one of the pleasures of age. The old *casus conscientiæ* of those in power—whether the weak tillage of an enfeebled hand ought not to be put up with in fields which have had the benefit of that hand's strength—arises less frequently now that the strength has often been expended elsewhere. The sojourning existence of the town masses is more and more

[37]

Life and Art

the existence of the rural masses, with its corresponding benefits and disadvantages. With uncertainty of residence often comes a laxer morality, and more cynical views of the duties of life. Domestic stability is a factor in conduct which nothing else can equal. On the other hand, new varieties of happiness evolve themselves like new varieties of plants, and new charms may have arisen among the classes who have been driven to adopt the remedy of locomotion for the evils of oppression and poverty—charms which compensate in some measure for the lost sense of home.

A practical injury which this wandering entails on the children of the labourers should be mentioned here. In shifting from school to school, their education cannot possibly progress with that regularity which is essential to their getting the best knowledge in the short time available to them. It is the remark of village school-teachers of experience, that the children of the vagrant workfolk form the mass of those who fail to reach the ordinary standard of knowledge expected of their age. The rural schoolmaster or mistress enters the schoolroom on the morning of the sixth of April, and finds that a whole flock of the brightest young people has suddenly flown away. In a village school which may be taken as a fair average specimen, containing seventy-five scholars, thirty-three vanished thus on the Lady Day of the present year. Some weeks elapse before the new comers drop in, and a longer time passes before they take root in the school, their dazed, unaccustomed mood rendering immediate progress impossible; while the original bright ones have by this time

The Dorsetshire Labourer

themselves degenerated into the dazed strangers of other districts.

That the labourers of the country are more independent since their awakening to the sense of an outer world cannot be disputed. It was once common enough on inferior farms to hear a farmer, as he sat on horseback amid a field of workers, address them with a contemptuousness which could not have been greatly exceeded in the days when the thralls of Cedric wore their collars of brass. Usually no answer was returned to these tirades; they were received as an accident of the land on which the listeners had happened to be born, calling for no more resentment than the blows of the wind and rain. But now, no longer fearing to avail himself of his privilege of flitting, these acts of contumely have ceased to be regarded as inevitable by the peasant. And while men do not of their own accord leave a farm without a grievance, very little fault-finding is often deemed a sufficient one among the younger and stronger. Such ticklish relations are the natural result of generations of unfairness on one side, and on the other an increase of knowledge, which has been kindled into activity by the exertions of Mr. Joseph Arch.

Nobody who saw and heard Mr. Arch in his early tours through Dorsetshire will ever forget him and the influence his presence exercised over the crowds he drew. He hailed from Shakespeare's county, where the humours of the peasantry have a marked family relationship with those of Dorset men; and it was this touch of nature, as much as his logic, which afforded him such

Life and Art

ready access to the minds and hearts of the labourers here. It was impossible to hear and observe the speaker for more than a few minutes without perceiving that he was a humourist—moreover, a man by no means carried away by an idea beyond the bounds of common sense. Like his renowned fellow-dalesman Corin, he virtually confessed that he was never in court, and might, with that eminent shepherd, have truly described himself as a 'natural philosopher,' who had discovered that 'he that wants money, means, and content, is without three good friends.'

'Content' may for a moment seem a word not exactly explanatory of Mr. Arch's views; but on the single occasion, several years ago, on which the present writer numbered himself among those who assembled to listen to that agitator, there was a remarkable moderation in his tone, and an exhortation to contentment with a reasonable amelioration, which, to an impartial auditor, went a long way in the argument. His views showed him to be rather the social evolutionist—what M. Emile de Laveleye would call a 'Possibilist'—than the anarchic irreconcilable. The picture he drew of a comfortable cottage life as it should be, was so cosy, so well within the grasp of his listeners' imagination, that an old labourer in the crowd held up a coin between his finger and thumb exclaiming, 'Here's zixpence towards that, please God!' 'Towards what?' said a bystander. 'Faith, I don't know that I can spak the name o't, but I know 'tis a good thing,' he replied.

The result of the agitation, so far, upon the income of the labourers, has been testified by independent witnesses with a unanimity which leaves no reasonable

The Dorsetshire Labourer

doubt of its accuracy. It amounts to an average rise of three shillings a week in wages nearly all over the county. The absolute number of added shillings seems small; but the increase is considerable when we remember that it is three shillings on eight or nine—*i.e.*, between thirty and forty per cent. And the reflection is forced upon everyone who thinks of the matter, that if a farmer can afford to pay thirty per cent. more wages in times of agricultural depression than he paid in times of agricultural prosperity, and yet live, and keep a carriage, while the landlord still thrives on the reduced rent which has resulted, the labourer must have been greatly wronged in those prosperous times. That the maximum of wage has been reached for the present is, however, pretty clear; and indeed it should be added that on several farms the labourers have submitted to a slight reduction during the past year, under stress of representations which have appeared reasonable.

It is hardly necessary to observe that the quoted wages never represent the labourer's actual income. Beyond the weekly payment—now standing at eleven or twelve shillings—he invariably receives a lump sum of 2*l.* or 3*l.* for harvest work. A cottage and garden is almost as invariably provided, free of rent, with, sometimes, an extra piece of ground for potatoes in some field near at hand. Fuel, too, is frequently furnished, in the form of wood faggots. At springtime, on good farms, the shepherd receives a shilling for every twin reared, while the carter gets what is called journey-money, that is, a small sum, mostly a shilling, for every journey taken beyond the bounds of the farm. Where all these supplementary trifles are enjoyed together, the

[41]

Life and Art

weekly wage in no case exceeds eleven shillings at the present time.

The question of enough or not enough often depends less upon the difference of two or three shillings a week in the earnings of the head of a family than upon the nature of his household. With a family of half a dozen children, the eldest of them delicate girls, nothing that he can hope to receive for the labour of his one pair of hands can save him from many hardships during a few years. But with a family of strong boys, of ages from twelve to seventeen or eighteen, he enjoys a season of prosperity. The very manner of the farmer towards him is deferential; for home-living boys, who in many cases can do men's work at half the wages, and without requiring the perquisites of house, garden-land, and so on, are treasures to the employer of agricultural labour. These precious lads are, according to the testimony of several respectable labourers, a more frequent cause of contention between employer and man than any other item in their reckonings. As the boys grow, the father asks for a like growth in their earnings; and disputes arise which frequently end in the proprietor of the valuables taking himself off to a farm where he and his will be better appreciated. The mother of the same goodly row of sons can afford to despise the farmer's request for female labour; she stays genteelly at home, and looks with some superciliousness upon wives who, having no useful children, are obliged to work in the fields like their husbands. A triumphant family of the former class, which recently came under notice, may be instanced. The father and eldest son were paid eleven shillings a week each, the younger son ten shillings,

The Dorsetshire Labourer

three nearly grown-up daughters four shillings a week
each, the mother the same when she chose to go out,
and all the women two shillings a week additional at
harvest; the men, of course, receiving their additional
harvest-money as previously stated, with house, garden,
and allotment free of charge. And since '*sine prole*'
would not frequently be written of the Dorset labourer
if his pedigree were recorded in the local history like
that of the other county families, such cases as the above
are not uncommon.

Women's labour, too, is highly in request, for a woman
who, like a boy, fills the place of a man at half the
wages, can be better depended on for steadiness. Thus
where a boy is useful in driving a cart or a plough, a
woman is invaluable in work which, though somewhat
lighter, demands thought. In winter and spring a farm-
woman's occupation is often 'turnip-hacking'—that is,
picking out from the land the stumps of turnips which
have been eaten off by the sheep—or feeding the thresh-
ing-machine, clearing away straw from the same, and
standing on the rick to hand forward the sheaves. In
mid-spring and early summer her services are required
for weeding wheat and barley (cutting up thistles and
other noxious plants with a spud), and clearing weeds
from pasture-land in like manner. In later summer
her time is entirely engrossed by haymaking—quite a
science, though it appears the easiest thing in the world
to toss hay about in the sun. The length to which a
skilful raker will work and retain command over her
rake without moving her feet is dependent largely upon
practice, and quite astonishing to the uninitiated.

Haymaking is no sooner over than the women are

hurried off to the harvest-field. This is a lively time. The bonus in wages during these few weeks, the cleanliness of the occupation, the heat, the cider and ale, influence to facetiousness and vocal strains. Quite the reverse do these lively women feel in the occupation which may be said to stand, emotionally, at the opposite pole to gathering in corn: that is, threshing it. Not a woman in the county but hates the threshing machine. The dust, the din, the sustained exertion demanded to keep up with the steam tyrant, are distasteful to all women but the coarsest. I am not sure whether, at the present time, women are employed to feed the machine, but some years ago a woman had frequently to stand just above the whizzing wire drum, and feed from morning to night—a performance for which she was quite unfitted, and many were the manœuvres to escape that responsible position. A thin saucer-eyed woman of fifty-five, who had been feeding the machine all day, declared on one occasion that in crossing a field on her way home in the fog after dusk, she was so dizzy from the work as to be unable to find the opposite gate, and there she walked round and round the field, bewildered and terrified, till three o'clock in the morning, before she could get out. The farmer said that the ale had got into her head, but she maintained that it was the spinning of the machine. The point was never clearly settled between them; and the poor woman is now dead and buried.

To be just, however, to the farmers, they do not enforce the letter of the Candlemas agreement in relation to the woman, if she makes any reasonable excuse for breaking it; and indeed, many a nervous farmer is put

The Dorsetshire Labourer

to flight by a matron who has a tongue with a tang, and who chooses to assert, without giving any reason whatever, that, though she had made fifty agreements, 'be cust if she will come out unless she is minded'—possibly terrifying him with accusations of brutality at asking her, when he knows 'how she is just now.' A farmer of the present essayist's acquaintance, who has a tendency to blush in the presence of beauty, and is in other respects a bashful man for his years, says that when the ladies of his farm are all together in a field, and he is the single one of the male sex present, he would as soon put his head into a hornet's nest as utter a word of complaint, or even a request beyond the commonest.

The changes which are so increasingly discernible in village life by no means originate entirely with the agricultural unrest. A depopulation is going on which in some quarters is truly alarming. Villages used to contain, in addition to the agricultural inhabitants, an interesting and better-informed class, ranking distinctly above those—the blacksmith, the carpenter, the shoemaker, the small higgler, the shopkeeper (whose stock-in-trade consisted of a couple of loaves, a pound of candles, a bottle of brandy-balls and lumps of delight, three or four scrubbing-brushes, and a frying-pan), together with nondescr:*t-workers other than farm-labourers, who had remained in the houses where they were born for no especial reason beyond an instinct of association with the spot. Many of these families had been life-holders, who built at their own expense the cottages they occupied, and as the lives dropped, and the property fell in they would have been glad to remain as weekly or monthly tenants of the owner. But the policy of all but some few philanthropic landowners is to disapprove of these petty tenants who are not in the estate's employ, and to pull down each cottage as it falls in, leaving standing a sufficient number for the use of the farmer's men and no more. The occupants who formed the back-bone of the village life have to seek refuge in the boroughs. This process, which is designated by statisticians as 'the tendency of the rural population towards the large towns,' is really the tendency of water to flow uphill when forced. The poignant regret of those who are thus obliged to forsake the old nest can only be realised by people who have witnessed it—concealed as it often is under a mask of indifference. It is anomalous that landowners who are showing unprecedented activity in the erection of comfortable cottages for their farm labourers, should see no reason for benefiting in the same way these unattached natives of the village who are nobody's care. They might often expostulate in the words addressed to King Henry the Fourth by his fallen subject:—

> Our house, my sovereign liege, little deserves
> The scourge of greatness to be used on it;
> And that same greatness, too, which our own hands
> Have holp to make so portly.

The system is much to be deplored, for every one of these banished people imbibes a sworn enmity to the existing order of things, and not a few of them, far from becoming merely honest Radicals, degenerate into Anarchists, waiters on chance, to whom danger to the

The Dorsetshire Labourer

State, the town—nay, the street they live in, is a wel‑
comed opportunity.

A reason frequently advanced for dismissing these
families from the villages where they have lived for
centuries is that it is done in the interests of morality;
and it is quite true that some of the 'liviers' (as these
half-independent villagers used to be called) were not
always shining examples of churchgoing, temperance,
and quiet walking. But a natural tendency to evil,
which develops to unlawful action when excited by contact with others like-minded, would often have remained
latent amid the simple isolated experiences of a village
life. The cause of morality cannot be served by com-
pelling a population hitherto evenly distributed over the
country to concentrate in a few towns, with the inevitable results of overcrowding and want of regular em-
ployment. But the question of the Dorset cottager here
merges in that of all the houseless and landless poor,
and the vast topic of the Rights of Man, to consider
which is beyond the scope of a merely descriptive
article.

The Rev. William Barnes, B.D.,
A Biographical Note

First appeared, as an obituary notice, in *The Athenaeum*, October 16, 1886.

U NTIL within the last year or two there were few figures more familiar to the eye in the county town of Dorset on a market day than an aged clergyman, quaintly attired in caped cloak, knee-breeches, and buckled shoes, with a leather satchel slung over his shoulders, and a stout staff in his hand. He seemed usually to prefer the middle of the street to the pavement, and to be thinking of matters which had nothing to do with the scene before him. He plodded along with a broad, firm tread, notwithstanding the slight stoop occasioned by his years. Every Saturday morning he might have been seen thus trudging up the narrow South Street, his shoes coated with mud or dust according to the state of the roads between his rural home and Dorchester, and a little grey dog at his heels, till he reached the four cross ways in the centre of the town. Halting here, opposite the public clock, he would pull his old-fashioned watch from its deep fob, and set it with great precision to London time. This, the invariable first act of his market visit, having been completed to his satisfaction, he turned round and methodically proceeded about his other business.

This venerable and well-characterized man was Wil-

The Rev. William Barnes, B.D.

liam Barnes, the Dorsetshire poet and philologer, by
whose death last week at the ripe age of eighty-six the
world has lost not only a lyric writer of a high order of
genius, but probably the most interesting link between
present and past forms of rural life that England possessed. The date of his birth at the very beginning of
the century is less explanatory of his almost unique position in this respect than the remoteness, even from contemporary provincial civilization, of the pastoral recesses in which his earlier years were passed—places
with whose now obsolete customs and beliefs his mind
was naturally imbued. To give one instance of the former tardiness of events in that part of the country: it
was a day almost within his remembrance when, amidst
the great excitement and applause of the natives, who
swept the street with brooms in honour of its arrival, a
stage coach made its first entry into Sturminster Newton, the little market town nearest to the hamlet of Bag-
bere, the home of his parents. And there used to come
to a little bridge, close to his father's door, till quite
recently, a conjuror or 'white wizard,' who cured af-
flicted persons by means of the toad-bag—a small piece
of linen having a limb from a living toad sewn up inside, to be worn round the sufferer's neck and next his
skin, the twitching movements of which limb gave, so it
was said, 'a turn' to the blood of the wearer, and effected
a radical change in his constitution.

Born so long ago as February 22nd, 1800 (1801 has
been given, but I believe incorrectly), amid such surroundings, a thorough son of the soil, and endowed with
great retentiveness and powers of observation, it is no
wonder that Barnes became a complete repertory of for-

gotten manners, words, and sentiments, a store which he afterwards turned to such good use in his writings on ancient British and Anglo-Saxon speech, customs, and folklore; above all, in the systematic study of his native dialect, as a result of which he has shown the world that far from being, as popularly supposed, a corruption of correct English, it is a distinct branch of Teutonic speech, regular in declension and conjugation, and richer in many classes of words than any other tongue known to him. As an instance of the latter he used to mention the pronouns with particular pride, there being no fewer than four demonstratives to set against the current English two. He would also instance any natural object, such as a tree, and show that there were double the number of names for its different parts in the Dorset dialect to those available in the standard tongue.

It was a proud day for young William Barnes when, some time in the year 1814 or 1815, a local solicitor, the late Mr. Dashwood, entered the village school and inquired if there was a boy clever enough with his pen to come and copy deeds in his office in a clerkly hand. The only lad who at all approximated to such a high description was Barnes, and the scene of testing him with the long quill pen and paper, and his selection by the lawyer, must have been one to which Mulready alone could have done justice. The youth thus found himself at a solicitor's desk, and, what was more, in a position to help himself in some degree to the grammars and glossaries his soul desired, and by whose diligent perusal at odd hours through many laborious years he became familiar with an astonishing number of languages and dialects. A more notable instance of self-help has seldom been re-

The Rev. William Barnes, B.D.

corded, considering the date in the century, the young man's circumstances, and the remote place of his residence, for it appears that he still lived on at the hamlet, walking to and from the town—or rather townlet —every day. In later years academic scholars were sometimes found to remark upon the unsystematic character of his linguistic attainments, but it cannot be gainsaid that he was almost always ready with definite and often exclusive information on whatever slightly known form of human speech might occur to the mind of his questioner, from Persian to Welsh, from the contemporary vernaculars of India to the tongues of the ancient British tribes. Over and above these subjects, his mind was occupied after his removal to Dorchester, to judge from his letters to old local newspapers, with investigations of Roman remains, theories on the origin of Stonehenge, and kindred archæological matters; while among his other hobbies about this time was engraving on wood and on silver, crests and initials upon old pieces of plate in the neighbourhood still remaining to testify to his skill in the art.

Though Barnes's first practical step in life had brought him to the office of a solicitor, his instincts were towards tuition; and when, some years later, he had become well settled in the county town he opened a school. As schoolmaster he was fairly successful from the first, and as time went by and he obtained, as a ten years' man, his university degree and took orders, the school grew highly popular. It was during this period—from early in the forties onwards—that he wrote at intervals the first, second, and third series of those sweet rustic poems by which his name will be best remembered.

Life and Art

He used to tell an amusing story of his experience on relinquishing the school at Dorchester to retire to the country rectory of Winterbourne Came, in which he has ended his days. About the very week of his translation, so to call it, the name of one of his pupils appeared in the *Times* and other papers at the head of the Indian examination list, a wide proportion of marks separating it from the name following. The novelty of these lists lent a keen interest to them in those days, and the next morning Mr. Barnes was deluged with letters from all parts of the country requesting him at almost any price to take innumerable sons, and produce upon them the same successful effect. 'I told them it took two to do it,' he would say, adding, 'Thus a popularity which I had never known during the working years of my life came at almost the first moment when it was no longer of use to me.'

To many readers of these pages the charming idyls known as Barnes's 'Poems in the Dorset Dialect' are too familiar to need description or eulogy. Though locally distinguished on the title-page by the name of the county at large, the chief scenes of their inspiration lie more precisely in the limited district to the north and north-west of Dorsetshire, that is to say in the secluded Vale of Blackmore, whose margin formed the horizon of his boyhood, and was, as he himself sings in one of the poems, the end of the world to him then. This fertile and sheltered tract of country, where the fields are never brown and the springs never dry, is bounded on the south by the bold chalk ridge that embraces the prominences of Hambledon Hill, Bulbarrow, Nettlecombe Tont, Dogbury, and High-Stoy. The prospect north-

The Rev. William Barnes, B.D.

wards from each of these heights is one which rivals, and in many points surpasses, those much admired views of Surrey and Buckinghamshire from Richmond Hill and the terrace at Windsor Castle, while the portion of the landscape immediately beneath the spectator is the abiding-place of the people whose daily doings, sayings, and emotions have been crystallized in the poet's verse. Occasionally, it is true, we find among the men and women presented in Mr. Barnes's volumes some who are housed in hamlets lying nominally beyond the Vale, but to my mind these characters are in a great measure Blackmore people away from home, bearing with them still the well-marked traits which distinguish the Vale population from that of the neighbouring uplands. The same may be said of his backgrounds and scenery. Moreover, when, moved by the pervading instinct of the nineteenth century, he gives us whole poems of still life, unaffected and realistic as a Dutch picture, the slow green river Stour of the same valley, with its deep pools, whence the trout leaps to the may-fly undisturbed by anglers, is found to be the stream dearest to his memory and the inspirer of some of his happiest effusions.

Unlike Burns, Béranger, and other poets of the people, Mr. Barnes never assumed the high conventional style; and he entirely leaves alone ambition, pride, despair, defiance, and other of the grander passions which move mankind great and small. His rustics are, as a rule, happy people, and very seldom feel the sting of the rest of modern mankind—the disproportion between the desire for serenity and the power of obtaining it. One naturally thinks of Crabbe in this connexion; but though they touch at points, Crabbe goes much further than

Life and Art

Barnes in questioning the justice of circumstance. Their pathos, after all, is the attribute upon which the poems must depend for their endurance; and the incidents which embody it are those of everyday cottage life, tinged throughout with that 'light that never was,' which the emotional art of the lyrist can project upon the commonest things. It is impossible to prophesy, but surely much English literature will be forgotten when 'Woak Hill' is still read for its intense pathos, 'Blackmore Maidens' for its blitheness, and 'In the Spring' for its Arcadian ecstasy.

Notwithstanding the wide appreciation of his verse both here and in America, so largely local were the poet's interests that it may be questioned if the enthusiasm which accompanied his own readings of his works in the town-halls of the shire was not more grateful to him than the admiration of a public he had never seen. The effect, indeed, of his recitations upon an audience well acquainted with the *nuances* of the dialect—impossible to impart to outsiders by any kind of translation—can hardly be imagined by readers of his lines acquainted only with English in its customary form. The poet's own mild smile at the boisterous merriment provoked by his droll delivery of such pieces as 'The Shy Man,' 'A Bit o' Sly Coorten,' and 'Dick and I' returns upon the memory as one of the most characteristic aspects of a man who was nothing if not genial; albeit that, while the tyranny of his audience demanded these broadly humorous productions, his own preferences were for the finer and more pathetic poems, such as 'Wife a-lost,' 'Woak Hill,' and 'Jaäy a-past.'

To those who knew Mr. Barnes in his prime it may

The Rev. William Barnes, B.D.

have been a matter for conjecture why a man of his energies should not at some point or other of his career have branched off from the quiet byways of his early manhood into the turmoils of the outer world, particularly as his tastes at that time were somewhat general, and the direction of his labours was dictated in the main by his opportunities. The explanation seems to be that the poetic side of his nature, though not always dominant, was but faintly ruled by the practical at any time, that his place-attachment was strong almost to a fault, and that his cosmopolitan interests, though lively, were always subordinate to those local hobbies and solicitudes whence came alike his special powers and his limitations.

Few young people who have seen him only in latter years, since the pallor and stoop of old age overcame him, can realize the robust, upright form of his middle life, the ruddy cheek, and the bright quick eye. The last, indeed, dimmed but slightly, and even on his death-bed his zest for the subject of speech-form was strong as ever. In one of his latest conversations he became quite indignant at the word 'bicycle.' 'Why didn't they call it "wheel-saddle"?' he exclaimed.

Though not averse to social intercourse, his friendships extended over but a small area of society. But those who, like the present writer, knew him well and long, entertained for him a warm affection; while casual visitors from afar were speedily won to kindly regard by the simplicity of his character, his forbearance, and the charming spurts of youthful ardour which would burst out as rays even in his latest hours.

[55]

The Profitable Reading of Fiction

First appeared in *The Forum* (New York), March, 1888.

WHEN the editor of this review courteously offered me space in his pages to formulate a few general notions upon the subject of novel reading, considered with a view to mental profit, I could not help being struck with the timeliness of the theme; for in these days the demand for novels has risen so high, in proportion to that for other kinds of literature, as to attract the attention of all persons interested in education. But I was by no means persuaded that one whose own writings have largely consisted in books of this class was in a position to say anything on the matter, even if he might be supposed to have anything to say. The field, however, is so wide and varied that there is plenty of room for impersonal points of regard; and I may as well premise that the remarks which follow, where not exclusively suggested by a consideration of the works of dead authors, are mere generalizations from a cursory survey, and no detailed analysis, of those of to-day.

If we speak of deriving good from a story, we usually mean something more than the gain of pleasure during the hours of its perusal. Nevertheless, to get pleasure out of a book is a beneficial and profitable thing, if the pleasure be of a kind which, while doing no moral injury, affords relaxation and relief when the mind is overstrained or sick of itself. The prime remedy in such

[56]

The Profitable Reading of Fiction

cases is change of scene, by which change of the material scene is not necessarily implied. A sudden shifting of the mental perspective into a fictitious world, combined with rest, is well known to be often as efficacious for renovation as a corporeal journey afar.

In such a case the shifting of scene should manifestly be as complete as if the reader had taken the hind seat on a witch's broomstick. The town man finds what he seeks in novels of the country, the countryman in novels of society, the indoor class generally in outdoor novels, the villager in novels of the mansion, the aristocrat in novels of the cottage.

The narrative must be of a somewhat absorbing kind, if not absolutely fascinating. To discover a book or books which shall possess, in addition to the special scenery, the special action required, may be a matter of some difficulty, though not always of such difficulty as to be insuperable; and it may be asserted that after every variety of spiritual fatigue there is to be found refreshment, if not restoration, in some antithetic realm of ideas which lies waiting in the pages of romance.

In reading for such hygienic purposes it is, of course, of the first consequence that the reader be not too critical. In other words, his author should be swallowed whole, like any other alterative pill. He should be believed in slavishly, implicitly. However profusely he may pour out his coincidences, his marvelous juxtapositions, his catastrophes, his conversions of bad people into good people at a stroke, and *vice versa,* let him never be doubted for a moment. When he exhibits people going out of their way and spending their money on purpose to act consistently, or taking a great deal of

Life and Art

trouble to move in a curious and roundabout manner when a plain, straight course lies open to them; when he shows that heroes are never faithless in love, and that the unheroic always are so, there should arise a conviction that this is precisely according to personal experience. Let the invalid reverse the attitude of a certain class of critics—now happily becoming less numerous—who only allow themselves to be interested in a novel by the defeat of every attempt to the contrary. The aim should be the exercise of a generous imaginativeness, which shall find in a tale not only all that was put there by the author, put he it never so awkwardly, but which shall find there what was never inserted by him, never foreseen, never contemplated. Sometimes these additions which are woven around a work of fiction by the intensitive power of the reader's own imagination are the finest parts of the scenery.

It is not altogether necessary to this tonic purpose that the stories chosen should be 'of most disastrous chances, of moving accidents by flood and field.' As stated above, the aim should be contrast. Directly the circumstances begin to resemble those of the reader, a personal connection, an interest other than an imaginative one, is set up, which results in an intellectual stir that is not in the present case to be desired. It sets his serious thoughts at work, and he does not want them stimulated just now; he wants to dream.

So much may be said initially upon alleviating the effects of over-work and carking care by a course of imaginative reading. But I will assume that benefit of this sort is not that which is primarily contemplated when we speak of getting good out of novels, but intel-

The Profitable Reading of Fiction

lectual or moral profit to active and undulled spirits.

It is obvious that choice in this case, though more limited than in the former, is by no means limited to compositions which touch the highest level in the essential constituents of a novel—those without which it would be no novel at all—the plot and the characters. Not only may the book be read for these main features—the presentation, as they may collectively be called—but for the accidents and appendages of narrative; and such are of more kinds than one. Excursions into various philosophies, which vary or delay narrative proper, may have more attraction than the regular course of the enactment; the judicious inquirer may be on the look-out for didactic reflection, such as is found in large lumps in 'Rasselas'; he may be a picker-up of trifles of useful knowledge, statistics, queer historic fact, such as sometimes occur in the pages of Hugo; he may search for specimens of the manners of good or bad society, such as are to be obtained from the fashionable writers; or he may even wish to brush up his knowledge of quotations from ancient and other authors by studying some chapters of 'Pelham' and the disquisitions of Parson Adams in 'Joseph Andrews.'

Many of the works which abound in appurtenances of this or a kindred sort are excellent as narrative, excellent as portraiture, even if in spite rather than in consequence of their presence. But they are the exception. Directly we descend from the highest levels we find that the majority are not effectual in their ostensible undertaking, that of giving us a picture of life in action; they exhibit a machinery which often works awkwardly, and at the instigation of unlikely beings. Yet, being packed

Life and Art

with thoughts of some solidity, or more probably sprinkled with smart observations on men and society, they may be read with advantage even by the critical, who, for what they bring, can forgive the audible working of the wheels and wires and carpentry, heard behind the performance, as the wires and trackers of a badly constructed organ are heard under its tones.

Novels of the latter class—formerly more numerous than now—are the product of cleverness rather than of intuition; and in taking them up—bearing in mind that profit, and not amusement, is the student's aim—his manifest course is to escape from the personages and their deeds, gathering the author's wit or wisdom nearly as it would have presented itself if he had cast his thoughts in the shape of an essay.

But though we are bound to consider by-motives like these for reading fiction as praiseworthy enough where practicable, they are by their nature of an illegitimate character, more or less, and apart from the ruling interest of the genuine investigator of this department of literature. Such ingredients can be had elsewhere in more convenient parcels. Our true object is a lesson in life, mental enlargement from elements essential to the narratives themselves and from the reflections they engender.

Among the qualities which appertain to representations of life, construed, though not distorted, by the light of imagination—qualities which are seldom shared by views *about* life, however profound—is that of self-proof or obviousness. A representation is less susceptible of error than a disquisition; the teaching, depending as it does upon intuitive conviction, and not upon logical reasoning, is not likely to lend itself to sophistry. If endowed with ordinary intelligence, the reader can discern, in delineative art professing to be natural, any stroke greatly at variance with nature, which, in the form of moral essay, *pensée*, or epigram, may be so wrapped up as to escape him.

Good fiction may be defined here as that kind of imaginative writing which lies nearest to the epic, dramatic, or narrative masterpieces of the past. One fact is certain: in fiction there can be no intrinsically new thing at this stage of the world's history. New methods and plans may arise and come into fashion, as we see them do; but the general theme can neither be changed, nor (what is less obvious) can the relative importance of its various particulars be greatly interfered with. The higher passions must ever rank above the inferior—intellectual tendencies above animal, and moral above intellectual—whatever the treatment, realistic or ideal. Any system of inversion which should attach more importance to the delineation of man's appetites than to the delineation of his aspirations, affections, or humors, would condemn the old masters of imaginative creation from Æschylus to Shakespeare. Whether we hold the arts which depict mankind to be, in the words of Mr. Matthew Arnold, a criticism of life, or, in those of Mr. Addington Symonds, a revelation of life, the material remains the same, with its sublimities, its beauties, its uglinesses, as the case may be. The finer manifestations must precede in importance the meaner, without such a radical change in human nature as we can hardly conceive as pertaining to an even remote future of decline, and certainly do not recognize now.

Life and Art

In pursuance of his quest for a true exhibition of man, the reader will naturally consider whether he feels himself under the guidance of a mind who sees further into life than he himself has seen; or, at least, who can throw a stronger irradiation over subjects already within his ken than he has been able to do unaided. The new light needs not to be set off by a finish of phraseology or incisive sentences of subtle definition. The treatment may be baldly incidental, without inference or commentary. Many elaborate reflections, for example, have been composed by moralizing chroniclers on the effect of prosperity in blunting men's recollection of those to whom they have sworn friendship when they shared a hard lot in common. But the writer in Genesis who tells his legend of certain friends in such adverse circumstances, one of whom, a chief butler, afterward came to good fortune, and ends the account of this good fortune with the simple words, 'Now the chief butler did not remember Joseph, but forgat him,' brings out a dramatic sequence on ground prepared for assent, shows us the general principle in the particular case, and hence writes with a force beyond that of aphorism or argument. It is the force of an appeal to the emotional reason rather than to the logical reason; for by their emotions men are acted upon, and act upon others.

If it be true, as is frequently asserted, that young people nowadays go to novels for their sentiments, their religion, and their morals, the question as to the wisdom or folly of those young people hangs upon their methods of acquisition in each case. A deduction from what these works exemplify by action that bears evidence of being a counterpart of life, has a distinct edu-

The Profitable Reading of Fiction

cational value; but an imitation of what may be called the philosophy of the personages—the doctrines of the actors, as shown in their conversation—may lead to surprising results. They should be informed that a writer whose story is not a tract in disguise has as his main object that of characterizing the people of his little world. A philosophy which appears between the inverted commas of a dialogue may, with propriety, be as full of holes as a sieve if the person or persons who advance it gain any reality of humanity thereby.

These considerations only bring us back again to the vital question how to discriminate the best in fiction. Unfortunately the two hundred years or so of the modern novel's development have not left the world so full of fine examples as to make it particularly easy to light upon them when the first obvious list has been run through. The, at first sight, high-piled granary sifts down to a very small measure of genuine corn. The conclusion cannot be resisted, notwithstanding what has been stated to the contrary in so many places, that the scarcity of perfect novels in any language is because the art of writing them is as yet in its youth, if not in its infancy. Narrative art is neither mature in its artistic aspect, nor in its ethical or philosophical aspect; neither in form nor in substance. To me, at least, the difficulties of perfect presentation in both these kinds appear of such magnitude that the utmost which each generation can be expected to do is to add one or two strokes toward the selection and shaping of a possible ultimate perfection.

In this scarcity of excellence in novels as wholes the reader must content himself with excellence in parts;

Life and Art

and his estimate of the degree to which any given modern instance approximates to greatness will, of course, depend not only upon the proportion that the finer characteristics bear to the mass, but upon the figure cut by those finer characteristics beside those of the admitted masterpieces as yet. In this process he will go with the professed critic so far as to inquire whether the story forms a regular structure of incident, accompanied by an equally regular development of character—a composition based on faithful imagination, less the transcript than the similitude of material fact. But the appreciative, perspicacious reader will do more than this. He will see what his author is aiming at, and by affording full scope to his own insight, catch the vision which the writer has in his eye, and is endeavoring to project upon the paper, even while it half eludes him.

He will almost invariably discover that, however numerous the writer's excellencies, he is what is called unequal; he has a specialty. This especial gift being discovered, he fixes his regard more particularly thereupon. It is frequently not that feature in an author's work which common repute has given him credit for; more often it is, while co-existent with his popular attribute, overshadowed by it lurking like a violet in the shade of the more obvious, possibly more vulgar, talent, but for which it might have received high attention. Behind the broad humor of one popular pen he discerns startling touches of weirdness; amid the colossal fancies of another he sees strokes of the most exquisite tenderness; and the unobtrusive quality may grow to have more charm for him than the palpable one.

The Profitable Reading of Fiction

It must always be borne in mind, despite the claims of realism, that the best fiction, like the highest artistic expression in other modes, is more true, so to put it, than history or nature can be. In history occur from time to time monstrosities of human action and character explicable by no known law which appertains to sane beings; hitches in the machinery of existence, wherein we have not yet discovered a principle, which the artist is therefore bound to regard as accidents, hinderances to clearness of presentation, and hence, weakeners of the effect. To take an example from sculpture: no real gladiator ever died in such perfect harmony with normal nature as is represented in the well-known Capitoline marble. There was always a jar somewhere, a jot or tittle of something foreign in the real death-scene, which did not essentially appertain to the situation, and tended toward neutralizing its pathos; but this the sculptor omitted, and so consecrated his theme. In drama likewise. Observe the characters of any sterling play. No dozen persons who were capable of being animated by the profound reasons and truths thrown broadcast over 'Hamlet' or 'Othello,' of feeling the pulse of life so accurately, ever met together in one place in this world to shape an end. And, to come to fiction, nobody ever met an Uncle Toby who was Uncle Toby all round; no historian's Queen Elizabeth was ever so perfectly a woman as the fictitious Elizabeth of 'Kenilworth.' What is called the idealization of characters is, in truth, the making of them too real to be possible.

It may seem something of a paradox to assert that the novels which most conduce to moral profit are likely to

Life and Art

be among those written without a moral purpose. But the truth of the statement may be realized if we consider that the didactic novel is so generally devoid of *vraisemblance* as to teach nothing but the impossibility of tampering with natural truth to advance dogmatic opinions. Those, on the other hand, which impress the reader with the inevitableness of character and environment in working out destiny, whether that destiny be just or unjust, enviable or cruel, must have a sound effect, if not what is called a good effect, upon a healthy mind.

Of the effects of such sincere presentation on weak minds, when the courses of the characters are not exemplary, and the rewards and punishments ill adjusted to deserts, it is not our duty to consider too closely. A novel which does moral injury to a dozen imbeciles, and has bracing results upon a thousand intellects of normal vigor, can justify its existence; and probably a novel was never written by the purest-minded author for which there could not be found some moral invalid or other whom it was capable of harming.

To distinguish truths which are temporary from truths which are eternal, the accidental from the essential, accuracies as to custom and ceremony from accuracies as to the perennial procedure of humanity, is of vital importance in our attempts to read for something more than amusement. There are certain novels, both among the works of living and the works of deceased writers, which give convincing proof of much exceptional fidelity, and yet they do not rank as great productions; for what they are faithful in is life garniture and not life. You are fully persuaded that the personages are clothed precisely as you see them clothed in the street, in the draw-

The Profitable Reading of Fiction

ing-room, at the assembly. Even the trifling accidents of their costume are rendered by the honest narrator. They use the phrases of the season, present or past, with absolute accuracy as to idiom, expletive, slang. They lift their tea-cups or fan themselves to date. But what of it, after our first sense of its photographic curiousness is past? In aiming at the trivial and the ephemeral they have almost surely missed better things. A living French critic goes even further concerning the novelists of social minutiæ. 'They are far removed,' says he, 'from the great imaginations which create and transform. They renounce free invention; they narrow themselves to scrupulous exactness; they paint clothes and places with endless detail.'

But we must not, as inquiring readers, fail to understand that attention to accessories has its virtues when the nature of its regard does not involve blindness to higher things; still more when it conduces to the elucidation of higher things. The writer who describes his type of a jeweled leader of society by saying baldly how much her diamonds cost at So-and-So's, what the largest of them weighed and measured, how it was cut and set, the particular style in which she wore her hair, cannot convey much profit to any class of readers save two—those bent on making a purchase of the like ornaments or of adorning themselves in the same fashion; and, a century hence, those who are studying the costumes and expenditure of the period. But, supposing the subject to be the same, let the writer be one who takes less of a broker's view of his heroine and her adornments; he may be worth listening to, though his simplicity be quite childlike. It is immaterial that our example is in verse:

Life and Art

Be you not proud of that rich hair
Which wantons with the love-sick air;
Whenas that ruby which you wear,
Sunk from the tip of your soft ear,
Will last to be a precious stone
When all your world of beauty's gone.—*Herrick*.

And thus we are led to the conclusion that, in respect of our present object, our concern is less with the subject treated than with its treatment. There have been writers of fiction, as of poetry, who can gather grapes of thorns and figs of thistles.

Closely connected with the humanizing education found in fictitious narrative which reaches to the level of an illuminant of life, is the æsthetic training insensibly given by familiarity with story which, presenting noth-ing exceptional in other respects, has the merit of being well and artistically constructed. To profit of this kind, from this especial source, very little attention has hith-erto been paid, though volumes have been written upon the development of the æsthetic sense by the study of painting and sculpture, and thus adding to the means of enjoyment. Probably few of the general body denomi-nated the reading public consider, in their hurried peru-sal of novel after novel, that, to a masterpiece in story there appertains a beauty of shape, no less than to a masterpiece in pictorial or plastic art, capable of giving to the trained mind an equal pleasure. To recognize this quality clearly when present, the construction of the plot, or fable, as it used to be called, is to be more par-ticularly observed than either in a reading for sentiments and opinions, or in a reading merely to discover the fates of the chief characters. For however real the persons,

[68]

The Profitable Reading of Fiction

however profound, witty, or humorous the observations, as soon as the book comes to be regarded as an exemplification of the art of story-telling, the story naturally takes the first place, and the example is not noteworthy as such unless the telling be artistically carried on.

The distinguishing feature of a well rounded tale has been defined in various ways, but the general reader need not be burdened with many definitions. Briefly, a story should be an organism. To use the words applied to the epic by Addison, whose artistic feeling in this kind was of the subtlest, 'nothing should go before it, be intermixed with it, or follow after it, that is not related to it.' Tested by such considerations as these there are obviously many volumes of fiction remarkable, and even great, in their character-drawing, their feeling, their philosophy, which are quite second-rate in their structural quality as narratives. Instances will occur to every one's mind; but instead of dwelling upon these it is more interesting to name some which most nearly fulfill the conditions. Their fewness is remarkable, and bears out the opinion expressed earlier in this essay, that the art of novel-writing is as yet in its tentative stage only. Among them 'Tom Jones' is usually pointed out as a near approach to perfection in this as in some other characteristics; though, speaking for myself, I do not perceive its great superiority in artistic form over some other novels of lower reputation. The 'Bride of Lammermoor' is an almost perfect specimen of form, which is the more remarkable in that Scott, as a rule, depends more upon episode, dialogue, and description, for exciting interest, than upon the well-knit interdependence of parts. And the first thirty chapters of 'Vanity Fair'

Life and Art

may be instanced as well-nigh complete in artistic presentation, along with their other magnificent qualities.

Herein lies Richardson's real if only claim to be placed on a level with Fielding: the artist spirit that he everywhere displays in the structural parts of his work and in the interaction of the personages, notably those of 'Clarissa Harlowe.' However cold, even artificial, we may, at times, deem the heroine and her companions in the pages of that excellent tale, however numerous the twitches of unreality in their movements across the scene beside those in the figures animated by Fielding, we feel, nevertheless, that we are under the guidance of a hand which has consummate skill in evolving a graceful, well-balanced set of conjectures, forming altogether one of those circumstantial wholes which, when approached by events in real life, cause the observer to pause and reflect, and say, 'What a striking history!' We should look generously upon his deficiency in the robuster touches of nature, for it is the deficiency of an author whose artistic sense of form was developed at the expense of his accuracy of observation as regards substance. No person who has a due perception of the constructive art shown in Greek tragic drama can be blind to the constructive art of Richardson.

I have dwelt the more particularly upon this species of excellence, not because I consider it to rank in quality beside truth of feeling and action, but because it is one which so few nonprofessional readers enjoy and appreciate without some kind of preliminary direction. It is usually the latest to be discerned by the novel consumer, and it is often never discerned by him or her at all. Every intelligent reader with a little experience of life

The Profitable Reading of Fiction

can perceive truth to nature in some degree; but a great reduction must be made for those who can trace in narrative the quality which makes the Apollo and the Aphrodite a charm in marble. Thoughtful readers are continually met with who have no intuition that such an attribute can be claimed by fiction, except in so far as it is included in style.

The indefinite word style may be made to express almost any characteristic of story-telling other than subject and plot, and it is too commonly viewed as being some independent, extraneous virtue or varnish with which the substance of a narrative is artificially overlaid. Style, as far as the word is meant to express something more than literary finish, can only be treatment, and treatment depends upon the mental attitude of the novelist; thus entering into the very substance of a narrative, as into that of any other kind of literature. A writer who is not a mere imitator looks upon the world with his personal eyes, and in his peculiar moods; thence grows up his style, in the full sense of the term.

> Cui lecta potenter erit res,
> Nec facundia deseret hunc, nec lucidus ordo.*

Those who would profit from the study of style should formulate an opinion of what it consists in by the aid of their own educated understanding, their perception of natural fitness, true and high feeling, sincerity, unhampered by considerations of nice collocation and balance of sentences, still less by conventionally accepted examples. They will make the discovery that certain names have, by some accident or other, grown to be regarded

* Hor. "De Arte Poetica," 40.

Life and Art

as of high, if not of supreme merit in the catalogue of exemplars, which have no essential claims, in this respect, to be rated higher than hundreds of the rank and file of literature who are never mentioned by critic or considered by reader in that connection. An author who has once acquired a reputation for style may write English down to the depths of slovenliness if he choose, without losing his character as a master; and this probably because, as before observed, the quality of style is so vague and inapprehensible as a distinct ingredient that it may always be supposed to be something else than what the reader perceives to be indifferent.

Considerations as to the rank or station in life from which characters are drawn can have but little value in regulating the choice of novels for literary reasons, and the reader may thus leave much to the mood of the moment. I remember reading a lecture on novels by a young and ingenious, though not very profound, critic, some years ago, in which the theory was propounded that novels which depict life in the upper walks of society must, in the nature of things, be better reading than those which exhibit the life of any lower class, for the reason that the subjects of the former represent a higher stage of development than their less fortunate brethren. At the first blush this was a plausible theory; but when practically tested it is found to be based on such a totally erroneous conception of what a novel is, and where it comes from, as not to be worth a moment's consideration. It proceeds from the assumption that a novel is the thing, and not a view of the thing. It forgets that the characters, however they may differ, express mainly the author, his largeness of heart or otherwise, his cul-

The Profitable Reading of Fiction

ture, his insight, and very little of any other living person, except in such an inferior kind of procedure as might occasionally be applied to dialogue, and would take the narrative out of the category of fiction: *i.e.*, verbatim reporting without selective judgment.

But there is another reason, disconnected entirely from methods of construction, why the physical condition of the characters rules nothing of itself one way or the other. All persons who have thoughtfully compared class with class—and the wider their experience the more pronounced their opinion—are convinced that education has as yet but little broken or modified the waves of human impulse on which deeds and words depend. So that in the portraiture of scenes in any way emotional or dramatic—the highest province of fiction—the peer and the peasant stand on much the same level; the woman who makes the satin train and the woman who wears it. In the lapse of countless ages, no doubt, improved systems of moral education will considerably and appreciably elevate even the involuntary instincts of human nature; but at present culture has only affected the surface of those lives with which it has come in contact, binding down the passions of those predisposed to turmoil as by a silken thread only, which the first ebullition suffices to break. With regard to what may be termed the minor key of action and speech—the unemotional, every-day doings of men—social refinement operates upon character in a way which is oftener than not prejudicial to vigorous portraiture, by making the exteriors of men their screen rather than their index, as with untutored mankind. Contrasts are disguised by the crust of conventionality, picturesqueness obliterated, and a subjective

[73]

Life and Art

system of description necessitated for the differentiation of character. In the one case the author's word has to be taken as to the nerves and muscles of his figures; in the other they can be seen as in an *écorché*.

The foregoing are a few imperfect indications how, to the best of my judgment, to discriminate fiction which will be the most desirable reading for the average man or woman of leisure, who does not wish the occupation to be wholly barren of results except in so far as it may administer to the pleasure of the hour. But, as with the horse and the stream in the proverb, no outside power can compel or even help a reader to gain good from such reading unless he has some natural eye for the finer qualities in the best productions of this class. It is unfortunately quite possible to read the most elevating works of imagination in our own or any language, and, by fixing the regard on the wrong sides of the subject, to gather not a grain of wisdom from them, nay, sometimes positive harm. What author has not had his experience of such readers?—the mentally and morally warped ones of both sexes, who will, where practicable, so twist plain and obvious meanings as to see in an honest picture of human nature an attack on religion, morals, or institutions. Truly has it been observed that 'the eye sees that which it brings with it the means of seeing.'

Candour in English Fiction

First appeared in *The New Review*, January, 1890. It was the third of a series of articles on this subject, the first two contributions having been presented by Walter Besant and E. Lynn Linton.

E VEN imagination is the slave of stolid circumstance; and the unending flow of inventiveness which finds expression in the literature of Fiction is no exception to the general law. It is conditioned by its surroundings like a river-stream. The varying character and strength of literary creation at different times may, indeed, at first sight seem to be the symptoms of some inherent, arbitrary, and mysterious variation; but if it were possible to compute, as in mechanics, the units of power or faculty, revealed and unrevealed, that exist in the world at stated intervals, an approximately even supply would probably be disclosed. At least there is no valid reason for a contrary supposition. Yet of the inequality in its realisations there can be no question; and the discrepancy would seem to lie in contingencies which, at one period, doom high expression to dumbness and encourage the lower forms, and at another call forth the best in expression and silence triviality.

That something of this is true has indeed been pretty generally admitted in relation to art-products of various other kinds. But when observers and critics remark, as

[75]

Life and Art

they often do remark, that the great bulk of English fiction of the present day is characterised by its lack of sincerity, they usually omit to trace this serious defect to external, or even eccentric causes. They connect it with an assumption that the attributes of insight, conceptive power, imaginative emotion, are distinctly weaker nowadays than at particular epochs of earlier date. This may or may not be the case to some degree; but, on considering the conditions under which our popular fiction is produced, imaginative deterioration can hardly be deemed the sole or even chief explanation why such an undue proportion of this sort of literature is in England a literature of quackery.

By a sincere school of Fiction we may understand a Fiction that expresses truly the views of life prevalent in its time, by means of a selected chain of action best suited for their exhibition. What are the prevalent views of life just now is a question upon which it is not necessary to enter further than to suggest that the most natural method of presenting them, the method most in accordance with the views themselves, seems to be by a procedure mainly impassive in its tone and tragic in its developments.

Things move in cycles; dormant principles renew themselves, and exhausted principles are thrust by. There is a revival of the artistic instincts towards great dramatic motives—setting forth that 'collision between the individual and the general'—formerly worked out with such force by the Periclean and Elizabethan dramatists, to name no other. More than this, the periodicity which marks the course of taste in civilised countries does not take the form of a true cycle of repetition, but

Candour in English Fiction

what Comte, in speaking of general progress, happily characterises as 'a looped orbit': not a movement of revolution but—to use the current word—evolution. Hence, in perceiving that taste is arriving anew at the point of high tragedy, writers are conscious that its revived presentation demands enrichment by further truths—in other words, original treatment: treatment which seeks to show Nature's unconsciousness not of essential laws, but of those laws framed merely as social expedients by humanity, without a basis in the heart of things; treatment which expresses the triumph of the crowd over the hero, of the commonplace majority over the exceptional few.

But originality makes scores of failures for one final success, precisely because its essence is to acknowledge no immediate precursor or guide. It is probably to these inevitable conditions of further acquisition that may be attributed some developments of naturalism in French novelists of the present day and certain crude results from meritorious attempts in the same direction by intellectual adventurers here and there among our own authors.

Anyhow, conscientious fiction alone it is which can excite a reflective and abiding interest in the minds of thoughtful readers of mature age, who are weary of puerile inventions and famishing for accuracy; who consider that, in representations of the world, the passions ought to be proportioned as in the world itself. This is the interest which was excited in the minds of the Athenians by their immortal tragedies, and in the minds of Londoners at the first performance of the finer plays of three hundred years ago. They reflected life, revealed

Life and Art

life, criticised life. Life being a physiological fact, its honest portrayal must be largely concerned with, for one thing, the relations of the sexes, and the substitution for such catastrophes as favour the false colouring best expressed by the regulation finish that 'they married and were happy ever after,' of catastrophes based upon sexual relationship as it is. To this expansion English society opposes a well-nigh insuperable bar.

The popular vehicles for the introduction of a novel to the public have grown to be, from one cause and another, the magazine and the circulating library; and the object of the magazine and circulating library is not upward advance but lateral advance; to suit themselves to what is called household reading, which means, or is made to mean, the reading of the majority in a household or of the household collectively. The number of adults, even in a large household, being normally two, and these being the members which, as a rule, have least time on their hands to bestow on current literature, the taste of the majority can hardly be, and seldom is, tempered by the ripe judgment which desires fidelity. However, the immature members of a household often keep an open mind, and they might, and no doubt would, take sincere fiction with the rest but for another condition, almost generally co-existent: which is that adults who would desire true views for their own reading insist, for a plausible but questionable reason, upon false views for the reading of their young people.

As a consequence, the magazine in particular and the circulating library in general do not foster the growth of the novel which reflects and reveals life. They directly

[78]

Candour in English Fiction

tend to exterminate it by monopolising all literary space. Cause and effect were never more clearly conjoined, though commentators upon the result, both French and English, seem seldom if ever to trace their connection. A sincere and comprehensive sequence of the ruling passions, however moral in its ultimate bearings, must not be put on paper as the foundation of imaginative works, which have to claim notice through the above-named channels, though it is extensively welcomed in the form of newspaper reports. That the magazine and library have arrogated to themselves the dispensation of fiction is not the fault of the authors, but of circumstances over which they, as representatives of Grub Street, have no control.

What this practically amounts to is that the patrons of literature—no longer Peers with a taste—acting under the censorship of prudery, rigorously exclude from the pages they regulate subjects that have been made, by general approval of the best judges, the bases of the finest imaginative compositions since literature rose to the dignity of an art. The crash of broken commandments is as necessary an accompaniment to the catastrophe of a tragedy as the noise of drum and cymbals to a triumphal march. But the crash of broken commandments shall not be heard; or, if at all, but gently, like the roaring of Bottom—gently as any sucking dove, or as 'twere any nightingale, lest we should fright the ladies out of their wits. More precisely, an arbitrary proclamation has gone forth that certain picked commandments of the ten shall be preserved intact—to wit, the first, third, and seventh; that the ninth

Life and Art

shall be infringed but gingerly; the sixth only as much as necessary; and the remainder alone as much as you please, in a genteel manner.

It is in the self-consciousness engendered by interference with spontaneity, and in aims at a compromise to square with circumstances, that the real secret lies of the charlatanry pervading so much of English fiction. It may be urged that abundance of great and profound novels might be written which should require no compromising, contain not an episode deemed questionable by prudes. This I venture to doubt. In a ramification of the profounder passions the treatment of which makes the great style, something 'unsuitable' is sure to arise; and then comes the struggle with the literary conscience. The opening scenes of the would-be great story may, in a rash moment, have been printed in some popular magazine before the remainder is written; as it advances month by month the situations develop, and the writer asks himself, what will his characters do next? What would probably happen to them, given such beginnings? On his life and conscience, though he had not foreseen the thing, only one event could possibly happen, and that therefore he should narrate, as he calls himself a faithful artist. But, though pointing a fine moral, it is just one of those issues which are not to be mentioned in respectable magazines and select libraries. The dilemma then confronts him, he must either whip and scourge those characters into doing something contrary to their natures, to produce the spurious effect of their being in harmony with social forms and ordinances, or, by leaving them alone to act as they will, he must bring down the thunders of re-

Candour in English Fiction

spectability upon his head, not to say ruin his editor, his publisher, and himself.

What he often does, indeed can scarcely help doing in such a strait, is, belie his literary conscience, do despite to his best imaginative instincts by arranging a *dénouement* which he knows to be indescribably unreal and meretricious, but dear to the Grundyist and subscriber. If the true artist ever weeps it probably is then, when he first discovers the fearful price that he has to pay for the privilege of writing in the English language—no less a price than the complete extinction, in the mind of every mature and penetrating reader, of sympathetic belief in his personages.

To say that few of the old dramatic masterpieces, if newly published as a novel (the form which, experts tell us, they would have taken in modern conditions), would be tolerated in English magazines and libraries is a ludicrous understatement. Fancy a brazen young Shakespeare of our time—'Othello,' 'Hamlet,' or 'Antony and Cleopatra' never having yet appeared—sending up one of those creations in narrative form to the editor of a London magazine, with the author's compliments, and his hope that the story will be found acceptable to the editor's pages; suppose him, further, to have the temerity to ask for the candid remarks of the accomplished editor upon his manuscript. One can imagine the answer that young William would get for his mad supposition of such fitness from any one of the gentlemen who so correctly conduct that branch of the periodical Press.*

* It is, indeed, curious to consider what great works of the past the notions of the present day would aim to exclude from circulation, if not from publication, if they were issued as new fiction. In addition to those

Life and Art

Were the objections of the scrupulous limited to a prurient treatment of the relations of the sexes, or to any view of vice calculated to undermine the essential principles of social order, all honest lovers of literature would be in accord with them. All really true literature directly or indirectly sounds as its refrain the words in the 'Agamemnon': 'Chant Ælinon, Ælinon! but may the good prevail.' But the writer may print the *not* of his broken commandment in capitals of flame; it makes no difference. A question which should be wholly a question of treatment is confusedly regarded as a question of subject.

Why the ancient classic and old English tragedy can be regarded thus deeply, both by young people in their teens and by old people in their moralities, and the modern novel cannot be so regarded; why the honest and uncompromising delineation which makes the old stories and dramas lessons in life must make of the modern novel, following humbly on the same lines, a lesson in iniquity, is to some thinkers a mystery inadequately accounted for by the difference between old and new.

Whether minors should read unvarnished fiction based on the deeper passions, should listen to the eternal verities in the form of narrative, is somewhat a different question from whether the novel ought to be exclusively addressed to those minors. The first consideration is

mentioned, think of the 'King Œdipus' of Sophocles, the 'Agamemnon' of Æschylus, Goethe's 'Faust' and 'Wilhelm Meister,' the 'Prometheus' of Æschylus, Milton's 'Paradise Lost.' The 'unpleasant subjects' of the two first-named compositions, the 'unsuitableness' of the next two, would be deemed equalled only by the profanity of the two last; for Milton, as it is hardly necessary to remind the reader, handles as his puppets the Christian divinities and fiends quite as freely as the Pagan divinities were handled by the Greek and Latin imaginative authors.

Candour in English Fiction

one which must be passed over here; but it will be conceded by most friends of literature that all fiction should not be shackled by conventions concerning budding womanhood, which may be altogether false. It behoves us then to inquire how best to circumvent the present lording of nonage over maturity, and permit the explicit novel to be more generally written.

That the existing magazine and book-lending system will admit of any great modification is scarcely likely. As far as the magazine is concerned it has long been obvious that as a vehicle for fiction dealing with human feeling on a comprehensive scale it is tottering to its fall; and it will probably in the course of time take up openly the position that it already covertly occupies, that of a purveyor of tales for the youth of both sexes, as it assumes that tales for those rather numerous members of society ought to be written.

There remain three courses by which the adult may find deliverance. The first would be a system of publication under which books could be bought and not borrowed, when they would naturally resolve themselves into classes instead of being, as now, made to wear a common livery in style and subject, enforced by their supposed necessities in addressing indiscriminately a general audience.

But it is scarcely likely to be convenient to either authors or publishers that the periodical form of publication for the candid story should be entirely forbidden, and in retaining the old system thus far, yet ensuring that the emancipated serial novel should meet the eyes of those for whom it is intended, the plan of publication as a *feuilleton* in newspapers read mainly

Life and Art

by adults might be more generally followed, as in France. In default of this, or co-existent with it, there might be adopted what, upon the whole, would perhaps find more favour than any with those who have artistic interests at heart, and that is, magazines for adults; exclusively for adults, if necessary. As an offshot there might be at least one magazine for the middle-aged and old.

There is no foretelling; but this (since the magazine form of publication is so firmly rooted) is at least a promising remedy, if English prudery be really, as we hope, only a parental anxiety. There should be no mistaking the matter, no half measures. *La dignité de la pensée,* in the words of Pascal, might then grow to be recognised in the treatment of fiction as in other things, and untrammelled adult opinion on conduct and theology might be axiomatically assumed and dramatically appealed to. Nothing in such literature should for a moment exhibit lax views of that purity of life upon which the well-being of society depends; but the position of man and woman in nature, and the position of belief in the minds of man and woman—things which everybody is thinking but nobody is saying—might be taken up and treated frankly.

The Science of Fiction

First appeared in *The New Review,* April, 1891. It was the third of a series of articles on this subject; the first two contributions were by Paul Bourget and Walter Besant.

SINCE Art is science with an addition, since some science underlies all Art, there is seemingly no paradox in the use of such a phrase as 'the Science of Fiction.' One concludes it to mean that comprehensive and accurate knowledge of realities which must be sought for, or intuitively possessed, to some extent, before anything deserving the name of an artistic performance in narrative can be produced.

The particulars of this science are the generals of almost all others. The materials of Fiction being human nature and circumstances, the science thereof may be dignified by calling it the codified law of things as they really are. No single pen can treat exhaustively of this. The Science of Fiction is contained in that large work, the cyclopædia of life.

In no proper sense can the term 'science' be applied to other than this fundamental matter. It can have no part or share in the construction of a story, however recent speculations may have favoured such an application. We may assume with certainty that directly the constructive stage is entered upon, Art—high or low—begins to exist.

The most devoted apostle of realism, the sheerest

naturalist, cannot escape, any more than the withered old gossip over her fire, the exercise of Art in his labour or pleasure of telling a tale. Not until he becomes an automatic reproducer of all impressions whatsoever can he be called purely scientific, or even a manufacturer on scientific principles. If in the exercise of his reason he select or omit, with an eye to being more truthful than truth (the just aim of Art), he transforms himself into a technicist at a move.

As this theory of the need for the exercise of the Dædalian faculty for selection and cunning manipulation has been disputed, it may be worth while to examine the contrary proposition. That it should ever have been maintained by such a romancer as M. Zola, in his work on the *Roman Expérimental,* seems to reveal an obtuseness to the disproof conveyed in his own novels which, in a French writer, is singular indeed. To be sure that author—whose powers in story-telling, rightfully and wrongfully exercised, may be partly owing to the fact that he is not a critic—does in a measure concede something in the qualified counsel that the novel should keep as close to reality *as it can;* a remark which may be interpreted with infinite latitude, and would no doubt have been cheerfully accepted by Dumas *père* or Mrs. Radcliffe. It implies discriminative choice; and if we grant that we grant all. But to maintain in theory what he abandons in practice, to subscribe to rules and to work by instinct, is a proceeding not confined to the author of 'Germinal' and 'La Faute de l'Abbé Mouret.'

The reasons that make against such conformation of story-writing to scientific processes have been set forth

The Science of Fiction

so many times in examining the theories of the realist, that it is not necessary to recapitulate them here. Admitting the desirability, the impossibility of reproducing in its entirety the phantasmagoria of experience with infinite and atomic truth, without shadow, relevancy, or subordination, is not the least of them. The fallacy appears to owe its origin to the just perception that with our widened knowledge of the universe and its forces, and man's position therein, narrative, to be artistically convincing, must adjust itself to the new alignment, as would also artistic works in form and colour, if further spectacles in their sphere could be presented. Nothing but the illusion of truth can permanently please, and when the old illusions begin to be penetrated, a more natural magic has to be supplied.

Creativeness in its full and ancient sense—the making a thing or situation out of nothing that ever was before —is apparently ceasing to satisfy a world which no longer believes in the abnormal—ceasing at least to satisfy the van-couriers of taste; and creative fancy has accordingly to give more and more place to realism, that is, to an artificiality distilled from the fruits of closest observation.

This is the meaning deducible from the work of the realists, however stringently they themselves may define realism in terms. Realism is an unfortunate, an ambiguous word, which has been taken up by literary society like a view-halloo, and has been assumed in some places to mean copyism, and in others pruriency, and has led to two classes of delineators being included in one condemnation.

Just as bad a word is one used to express a conse-

Life and Art

quence of this development, namely 'brutality,' a term which, first applied by French critics, has since spread over the English school like the other. It aptly hits off the immediate impression of the thing meant; but it has the disadvantage of defining impartiality as a passion, and a plan as a caprice. It certainly is very far from truly expressing the aims and methods of conscientious and well-intentioned authors who, notwithstanding their excesses, errors, and rickety theories, attempt to narrate the *vérité vraie*.

To return for a moment to the theories of the scientific realists. Every friend to the novel should and must be in sympathy with their error, even while distinctly perceiving it. Though not true, it is well found. To advance realism as complete copyism, to call the idle trade of story-telling a science, is the hyperbolic flight of an admirable enthusiasm, the exaggerated cry of an honest reaction from the false, in which the truth has been impetuously approached and overleapt in fault of lighted on.

Possibly, if we only wait, the third something, akin to perfection, will exhibit itself on its due pedestal. How that third something may be induced to hasten its presence, who shall say? Hardly the English critic.

But this appertains to the Art of novel-writing, and is outside the immediate subject. To return to the 'science.' . . . Yet what is the use? Its very comprehensiveness renders the attempt to dwell upon it a futility. Being an observative responsiveness to everything within the cycle of the suns that has to do with actual life, it is easier to say what it is not than to categorise its *summa genera*. It is not, for example,

The Science of Fiction

the paying of a great regard to adventitious externals to the neglect of vital qualities, not a precision about the outside of the platter and an obtuseness to the contents. An accomplished lady once confessed to the writer that she could never be in a room two minutes without knowing every article of furniture it contained and every detail in the attire of the inmates, and, when she left, remembering every remark. Here was a person, one might feel for the moment, who could prime herself to an unlimited extent and at the briefest notice in the scientific data of fiction; one who, assuming her to have some slight artistic power, was a born novelist. To explain why such a keen eye to the superficial does not imply a sensitiveness to the intrinsic is a psychological matter beyond the scope of these notes; but that a blindness to material particulars often accompanies a quick perception of the more ethereal characteristics of humanity, experience continually shows.

A sight for the finer qualities of existence, an ear for the 'still sad music of humanity,' are not to be acquired by the outer senses alone, close as their powers in photography may be. What cannot be discerned by eye and ear, what may be apprehended only by the mental tactility that comes from a sympathetic appreciativeness of life in all its manifestations, this is the gift which renders its possessor a more accurate delineator of human nature than many another with twice his powers and means of external observation, but without that sympathy. To see in half and quarter views the whole picture, to catch from a few bars the whole tune, is the intuitive power that supplies the would-be story-writer with the scientific bases for his pursuit. He may not

Life and Art

count the dishes at a feast, or accurately estimate the value of the jewels in a lady's diadem; but through the smoke of those dishes, and the rays from these jewels, he sees written on the wall:—

> We are such stuff
> As dreams are made of, and our little life
> Is rounded with a sleep.

Thus, as aforesaid, an attempt to set forth the Science of Fiction in calculable pages is futility; it is to write a whole library of human philosophy, with instructions how to feel.

Once in a crowd a listener heard a needy and illiterate women saying of another poor and haggard woman who had lost her little son years before: 'You can see the ghost of that child in her face even now.'

That speaker was one who, though she could probably neither read nor write, had the true means towards the 'Science' of Fiction innate within her; a power of observation informed by a living heart. Had she been trained in the technicalities, she might have fashioned her view of mortality with good effect; a reflection which leads to a conjecture that, perhaps, true novelists, like poets, are born, not made.

Memories of Church Restoration

Read at the General Meeting of the Society for
the Protection of Ancient Buildings, June 20,
1906. Published in the *Cornhill Magazine*, July,
1906.

A MELANCHOLY reflection may have occurred
to many people whose interests lie in the study
of Gothic architecture. The passion for 'restoration' first became vigorously operative, say, three-
quarters of a century ago; and if all the mediæval buildings in England had been left as they stood at that date,
to incur whatever dilapidations might have befallen them
at the hands of time, weather, and general neglect, this
country would be richer in specimens to-day than it finds
itself to be after the expenditure of millions in a nomi-
nal preservation during that period.

Active destruction under saving names has been effected upon so gigantic a scale that the concurrent protection of old structures, or portions of structures, by
their being kept wind- and water-proof amid such operations counts as nothing in the balance. Its enormous
magnitude is realised by few who have not gone personally from parish to parish through a considerable district, and compared existing churches there with records,
traditions, and memories of what they formerly were.

But the unhappy fact is nowadays generally admitted,
and it would hardly be worth adverting to on this occasion if what is additionally assumed were also true, or

Life and Art

approximately true: that we are wiser with experience, that architects, incumbents, church-wardens, and all concerned, are zealous to act conservatively by such few of these buildings as still remain untinkered, that they desire at last to repair as far as is possible the errors of their predecessors, and to do anything but repeat them.

Such an assumption is not borne out by events. As it was in the days of Scott the First and Scott the Second —Sir Walter and Sir Gilbert—so it is at this day on a smaller scale. True it may be that our more intelligent architects now know the better way, and that damage is largely limited to minor buildings and to obscure places. But continue it does, despite the efforts of this society; nor does it seem ever likely to stop till all tampering with chronicles in stone be forbidden by law, and all operations bearing on their repair be permitted only under the eyes of properly qualified inspectors.

At first sight it seems an easy matter to preserve an old building without hurting its character. Let nobody form an opinion on that point who has never had an old building to preserve.

In respect of an ancient church, the difficulty we encounter on the threshold, and one which besets us at every turn, is the fact that the building is beheld in two contradictory lights, and required for two incompatible purposes. To the incumbent the church is a workshop; to the antiquary it is a relic. To the parish it is a utility; to the outsider a luxury. How unite these incompatibles? A utilitarian machine has naturally to be kept going, so that it may continue to discharge its original functions; an antiquarian specimen has to be preserved without making good even its worst deficiencies. The

Memories of Church Restoration

quaintly carved seat that a touch will damage has to be sat in, the frameless doors with the queer old locks and hinges have to keep out draughts, the bells whose shaking endangers the graceful steeple have to be rung.

If the ruinous church could be enclosed in a crystal palace, covering it to the weathercock from rain and wind, and a new church be built alongside for services (assuming the parish to retain sufficient earnest-mindedness to desire them), the method would be an ideal one. But even a parish composed of opulent members of this society would be staggered by such an undertaking. No: all that can be done is of the nature of compromise. It is not within the scope of this paper to inquire how such compromises between users and musers may best be carried out, and how supervision, by those who really know, can best be ensured when wear and tear and the attacks of weather make interference unhappily unavoidable. Those who are better acquainted than I am with the possibilities of such cases can write thereon, and have, indeed, already done so for many years past. All that I am able to do is to look back in a contrite spirit at my own brief experience as a church-restorer, and, by recalling instances of the drastic treatment we then dealt out with light hearts to the unlucky fanes that fell into our hands, possibly help to prevent its repetition on the few yet left untouched.

The policy of thoroughness in these proceedings was always, of course, that in which the old church was boldly pulled down from no genuine necessity, but from a wanton wish to erect a more modish one. Instances of such I pass over in sad silence. Akin thereto was the case in which a church exhibiting two or three styles was made

Life and Art

uniform by removing the features of all but one style, and imitating that throughout in new work. Such devastations need hardly be dwelt on now. Except in the most barbarous recesses of our counties they are past. Their name alone is their condemnation.

The shifting of old windows, and other details irregularly spaced, and spacing them at exact distances, was an analogous process. The deportation of the original chancel-arch to an obscure nook, and the insertion of a wider new one to throw open the view of the choir, was also a practice much favoured, and is by no means now extinct. In passing through a village less than five years ago the present writer paused a few minutes to look at the church, and on reaching the door heard quarrelling within. The voices were discovered to be those of two men—brothers, I regret to state—who after an absence of many years had just returned to their native place to attend their father's funeral. The dispute was as to where the family pew had stood in their younger days. One swore that it was in the north aisle, adducing as proof his positive recollection of studying Sunday after Sunday the zigzag moulding of the arch before his eyes, which now visibly led from that aisle into the north transept. The other was equally positive that the pew had been in the nave. As the altercation grew sharper an explanation of the puzzle occurred to me, and I suggested that the old Norman arch we were looking at might have been the original chancel-arch, banished into the aisle to make room for the straddling new object in its place. Then one of the pair of natives remembered that a report of such a restoration had reached his ears afar, and the family peace was preserved, though not till the other had said, 'Then I'm drowned if I'll ever come into the paltry church again, after having such a trick played upon me.'

Many puzzling questions are to be explained by these shiftings, and particularly in the case of monuments, whose transposition sometimes led to quaint results. The chancel of a church not a hundred and fifty miles from London has, I am told, in one corner a vault containing a fashionable actor and his wife, in another corner a vault inclosing the remains of a former venerable vicar who abjured women and died a bachelor. The mural tablets, each over its own vault, were taken down at the refurbishing of the building, and refixed reversely, the stone of the theatrical couple over the solitary divine, and that of the latter over the pair from the stage. Should disinterment ever take place, which is not unlikely nowadays, the excavators will be surprised to find a lady beside the supposed reverend bachelor, and the supposed actor without his wife. As the latter was a comedian he would probably enjoy the situation if he could know it, though the vicar's feelings might be somewhat different.

Such facetious carelessness is not peculiar to our own country. It may be remembered that when Mrs. Shelley wished to exhume her little boy William, who had been buried in the English cemetery at Rome, with the view of placing his body beside his father's ashes, no coffin was found beneath the boy's headstone, and she could not carry out her affectionate wish.

This game of Monumental Puss-in-the-Corner, even when the outcome of no blundering, and where reasons can be pleaded on artistic or other grounds, is, indeed,

Life and Art

an unpleasant subject of contemplation by those who maintain the inviolability of records. Instances of such in London churches will occur to everybody. One would like to know if any note has been kept of the original position of Milton's monument in Cripplegate Church, which has been moved more than once, I believe, and if the position of his rifled grave is now known. When I first saw the monument it stood near the east end of the south aisle.

Sherborne Abbey affords an example on a large scale of the banishment of memorials of the dead, to the doubtful advantage of the living. To many of us the human interest in an edifice ranks before its architectural interest, however great the latter may be; and to find that the innumerable monuments erected in that long-suffering building are all huddled away into the vestry is, at least from my point of view, a heavy mental payment for the clear nave and aisles. If the inscriptions could be read the harm would perhaps be less, but to read them is impossible without ladders, so that these plaintive records are lost to human notice. Many of the recorded ones, perhaps, deserve to be forgotten; but who shall judge?

And unhappily it was oftenest of all the headstones of the poorer inhabitants—purchased and erected in many cases out of scanty means—that suffered most in these ravages. It is scarcely necessary to particularise among the innumerable instances in which headstones have been removed from their positions, the churchyard levelled, and the stones used for paving the churchyard walks, with the result that the inscriptions have been trodden out in a few years.

Memories of Church Restoration

Next in harm to the re-designing of old buildings and parts of them came the devastations caused by letting restorations by contract, with a clause in the specification requesting the builder to give a price for 'old materials'—the most important of these being the lead of the roofs, which was to be replaced by tiles or slate, and the oaks of the pews, pulpit, altar-rails, &c., to be replaced by deal. This terrible custom is, I should suppose, discontinued in these days. Under it the builder was directly incited to destroy as much as possible of the old fabric as had intrinsic value, that he might increase the spoil which was to come to him for a fixed deduction from his contract. Brasses have marvellously disappeared at such times, heavy brass chandeliers, marble tablets, oak carving of all sorts, leadwork above all.

But apart from irregularities it was always a principle that anything later than Henry VIII. was Anathema, and to be cast out. At Wimborne Minster fine Jacobean canopies were removed from Tudor stalls for the offence only of being Jacobean. At an hotel in Cornwall, a tea-garden was, and possibly is still, ornamented with seats constructed of the carved oak from a neighbouring church—no doubt the restorer's honest perquisite. Church relics turned up in unexpected places. I remember once going into the stonemason's shed of a builder's yard, where, on looking round, I started to see the Creed, the Lord's Prayer, and the Ten Commandments, in gilt letters, staring emphatically from the sides of the shed. 'Oh, yes,' said the builder, a highly respectable man, 'I took 'em as old materials under my contract when I gutted St. Michael and All Angels', and

[97]

Life and Art

I put 'em here to keep out the weather: they might keep
my blackguard hands serious at the same time; but they
don't.' A fair lady with a past was once heard to say
that she could not go to morning service at a particular
church because the parson read one of the Commandments with such accusatory emphasis: whether these that
had become degraded to the condition of old material
were taken down owing to kindred objections one cannot know.

But many such old materials were, naturally, useless
when once unfixed. Another churchwright whom I knew
in early days was greatly incommoded by the quantity
of rubbish that had accumulated during a restoration he
had in hand, there being no place in the churchyard to
which it could be wheeled. In the middle of the church
was the huge vault of an ancient family supposed to be
extinct, which had been broken into at one corner by
the pickaxe of the restorers, and this vault was found
to be a convenient receptacle for the troublesome refuse
from the Ages. When a large number of barrow-loads
had been tipped through the hole the labourer lifted his
eyes to behold a tall figure standing between him and the
light. 'What are you doing, my man?' said the figure
blandly. 'A getting rid of the rubbage, sir,' replied the
labourer. 'But why do you put it there?' 'Because all
the folks have died out, so it don't matter what we do
with their old bone cellar.' 'Don't you be too sure about
the folks having died out. I am one of that family, and
as I am very much alive, and that vault is my freehold,
I'll just ask you to take all the rubbish out again.' It
was said that the speaker had by chance returned from
America, where he had made a fortune, in the nick of

[98]

Memories of Church Restoration

time to witness this performance, and that the vault was duly cleared and sealed up as he ordered.

The 'munificent contributor' to the expense of restoration was often the most fearful instigator of mischief. I may instance the case of a Transition-Norman pier with a group of shafts, the capitals of which showed signs of crushing under the weight of the arches. By taking great care it was found possible to retain the abacus and projecting parts supporting it, sculptured with the vigorous curled leaves of the period, only the diminishing parts, or the bell of each capital, being renewed. The day after the re-opening of the church the lady who had defrayed much of the expense complained to the contractor of his mean treatment of her in leaving half the old capitals when he should have behaved handsomely, and renewed the whole. To oblige her the carver chipped over the surface of the old carving, not only in that pier, but in *all* the piers, and made it look as good as new.

Poor forlorn parishes, which could not afford to pay a clerk of works to superintend the alterations, suffered badly in these ecclesiastical convulsions. During the years they were raging at their height I journeyed to a distant place to supervise a case, in the enforced absence of an older eye. The careful repair of an interesting Early English window had been specified; but it was gone. The contractor, who had met me on the spot, replied genially to my gaze of concern: 'Well now, I said to myself when I looked at the old thing, "I won't stand upon a pound or two: I'll give 'em a new winder now I am about it, and make a good job of it, howsomever." ' A caricature in new stone of the old window had taken its place.

Life and Art

In the same church was an old oak rood-screen of debased Perpendicular workmanship, but valuable, the original colouring and gilding, though much faded, still remaining on the cusps and mouldings. The repairs deemed necessary had been duly specified, but I beheld in its place a new screen of deal, varnished to a mirror-like brilliancy. 'Well,' replied the builder, more genially than ever, 'I said to myself, "Please God, now I am about it, I'll do the thing well, cost what it will!"' 'Where's the old screen?' I said, appalled. 'Used up to boil the workmen's kittles; though 'a were not much at that!'

The reason for consternation lay in the fact that the bishop—a strict Protestant—had promulgated a decree concerning rood-screens—viz., that though those in existence might be repaired, no new one would be suffered in his diocese for doctrinal reasons. This the builder knew nothing of. What was to be done at the re-opening, when the bishop was to be present, and would notice the forbidden thing? I had to decide there and then, and resolved to trust to chance and see what happened. On the day of the opening we anxiously watched the bishop's approach, and I fancied I detected a lurid glare in his eye as it fell upon the illicit rood-screen. But he walked quite innocently under it without noticing that it was not the original. If he noticed it during the service he was politic enough to say nothing.

I might dwell upon the mistakes of architects as well as of builders if there were time. That architects the most experienced could be cheated to regard an accident of churchwardenry as high artistic purpose, was revealed to a body of architectural students, of which the present

Memories of Church Restoration

writer was one, when they were taken over Westminster Abbey in a peripatetic lecture by Sir Gilbert Scott. He, at the top of the ladder, was bringing to our notice a feature which had, he said, perplexed him for a long time: why the surface of diapered stone before him should suddenly be discontinued at the spot he pointed out, when there was every reason for carrying it on. Possibly the artist had decided that to break the surface was a mistake; possibly he had died; possibly anything; but there the mystery was. 'Perhaps it is only plastered over!' broke forth in the reedy voice of the youngest pupil in our group. 'Well, that's what I never thought of,' replied Sir Gilbert, and taking from his pocket a clasp knife which he carried for such purposes, he prodded the plain surface with it. 'Yes, it *is* plastered over, and all my theories are wasted,' he continued, descending the ladder not without humility.

My knowledge at first hand of the conditions of church-repair at the present moment is very limited. But one or two prevalent abuses have come by accident under my notice. The first concerns the rehanging of church bells. A barbarous practice is, I believe, very general, that of cutting off the cannon of each bell—namely, the loop on the crown by which it has been strapped to the stock—and restrapping it by means of holes cut through the crown itself. The mutilation is sanctioned on the ground that, by so fixing it, the centre of the bell's gravity is brought nearer to the axis on which it swings, with advantage and ease to the ringing. I do not question the truth of this; yet the resources of mechanics are not so exhausted but that the same result may be obtained by leaving the bell unmutilated and increasing the chamber of the stock, which, for that matter, might be so great as nearly to reach a right angle. I was recently passing through a churchyard where I saw standing on the grass a peal of bells just taken down from the adjacent tower and subjected to this treatment. A sight more piteous than that presented by these fine bells, standing disfigured in a row in the sunshine, like cropped criminals in the pillory, as it were ashamed of their degradation, I have never witnessed among inanimate things.

Speaking of bells, I should like to ask cursorily why the old sets of chimes have been removed from nearly all our country churches. The midnight wayfarer, in passing along the sleeping village or town, was cheered by the outburst of a stumbling tune, which possessed the added charm of being probably heeded by no ear but his own. Or, when lying awake in sickness, the denizen would catch the same notes, persuading him that all was right with the world. But one may go half across England and hear no chimes at midnight now.

I may here mention a singular incident in respect of a new peal of bells, at a church whose rebuilding I was privy to, which occurred on the opening day many years ago. It being a popular and fashionable occasion, the church was packed with its congregation long before the bells rang out for service. When the ringers seized the ropes, a noise more deafening than thunder resounded from the tower in the ears of the sitters. Terrified at the idea that the tower was falling, they rushed out at the door, ringers included, into the arms of the astonished bishop and clergy, advancing, so it was said, in procession up the churchyard path, some of the ladies being in a fainting state. When calmness was restored

Memories of Church Restoration

by the sight of the tower standing unmoved as usual, it was discovered that the six bells had been placed 'in stay'—that is, in an inverted position ready for the ringing, but in the hurry of preparation the clappers had been laid inside though not fastened on, and at the first swing of the bells they had fallen out upon the belfry floor.

After this digression I return to one other abuse of ecclesiastical fabrics, that arising from the fixing of Christmas decorations. The battalion of young ladies to whom the decking with holly and ivy is usually entrusted, seem to be possessed with a fixed idea that nails may be driven not only into old oak and into the joints of the masonry, but into the freestone itself if you only hit hard enough. Many observers must have noticed the mischief wrought by these nails. I lately found a fifteenth-century arch to have suffered more damage during the last twenty years from this cause than during the previous five hundred of its existence. The pock-marked surface of many old oak pulpits is entirely the effect of the numberless tin-tacks driven into them for the same purpose.

Such abuses as these, however, are gross, open, palpable, and easy to be checked. Far more subtle and elusive ones await our concluding consideration, which I will rapidly enter on now. Persons who have mused upon the safeguarding of our old architecture must have indulged in a reflection which, at first sight, seems altogether to give away the argument for its material preservation. The reflection is that, abstractly, there is everything to be said in favour of church renovation—if that really means the honest reproduction of old shapes in

Life and Art

substituted materials. And this too, not merely when the old materials are perishing, but when they are only approaching decay.

It is easy to show that the essence and soul of an architectural monument does not lie in the particular blocks of stone or timber that compose it, but in the mere forms to which those materials have been shaped. We discern in a moment that it is in the boundary of a solid —its insubstantial superficies or mould—and not in the solid itself, that its right lies to exist as art. The whole quality of Gothic or other architecture—let it be a cathedral, a spire, a window, or what not—attaches to this, and not to the substantial erection which it appears exclusively to consist in. Those limestones or sandstones have passed into its form; yet it is an idea independent of them—an æsthetic phantom without solidity, which might just as suitably have chosen millions of other stones from the quarry whereon to display its beauties. Such perfect results of art as the aspect of Salisbury Cathedral from the northeast corner of the Close, the interior of Henry VII.'s Chapel at Westminster, the East Window of Merton Chapel, Oxford, would be no less perfect if at this moment, by the wand of some magician, other similar materials could be conjured into their shapes, and the old substance be made to vanish for ever.

This is, indeed, the actual process of organic nature herself, which is one continuous substitution. She is always discarding the matter, while retaining the form.

Why this reasoning does not hold good for a dead art, why the existence and efforts of this Society are so amply justifiable, lies in two other attributes of bygone Gothic

Memories of Church Restoration

artistry—a material and a spiritual one. The first is uniqueness; such a duplicate as we have been considering can never be executed. No man can make two pieces of matter exactly alike. But not to shelter the argument behind microscopic niceties, or to imagine what approximations might be effected by processes so costly as to be prohibitive, it is found in practice that even such an easily copied shape as, say, a traceried window does not get truly reproduced. The old form inherits, or has acquired, an indefinable quality—possibly some deviation from exact geometry (curves were often struck by hand in mediæval work)—which never reappears in the copy, especially in the vast majority of cases where no nice approximation is attempted.

The second, or spiritual, attribute which stultifies the would-be reproducer is perhaps more important still, and is not artistic at all. It lies in human association. The influence that a building like Lincoln or Winchester exercises on a person of average impressionableness and culture is a compound influence, and though it would be a fanciful attempt to define how many fractions of that compound are æsthetic, and how many associative, there can be no doubt that the latter influence is more valuable than the former. Some may be of a different opinion, but I think the damage done to this sentiment of association by replacement, by the rupture of continuity, is mainly what makes the enormous loss this country has sustained from its seventy years of church restoration so tragic and deplorable. The protection of an ancient edifice against renewal in fresh materials is, in fact, even more of a social—I may say a humane—duty than an æsthetic one. It is the preservation of memories,

Life and Art

history, fellowships, fraternities. Life, after all, is more than art, and that which appealed to us in the (maybe) clumsy outlines of some structure which had been looked at and entered by a dozen generations of ancestors out-weighs the more subtle recognition, if any, of architectural qualities. The renewed stones at Hereford, Peterborough, Salisbury, St. Albans, Wells, and so many other places, are not the stones that witnessed the scenes in English Chronicle associated with those piles. They are not the stones over whose face the organ notes of centuries 'lingered and wandered on as loth to die,' and the fact that they are not, too often results in spreading abroad the feeling I instanced in the anecdote of the two brothers.

Moreover, by a curious irony, the parts of a church that have suffered the most complete obliteration are those of the closest personal relation—the woodwork, especially that of the oak pews of various Georgian dates, with their skilful panellings, of which not a joint had started, and mouldings become so hard as to turn the edge of a knife. The deal benches with which these cunningly mitred and morticed framings have been largely replaced have already, in many cases, fallen into decay.

But not all pewing was of oak, not all stonework and roof timbers were sound, when the renovators of the late century laid hands on them; and this leads back again to the standing practical question of bewildering difficulty which faces the protectors of Ancient Buildings—what is to be done in instances of rapid decay to prevent the entire disappearance of such as yet exists? Shall we allow it to remain untouched for the brief years of its durability, to have the luxury of the original a little while, or

[106]

Memories of Church Restoration

sacrifice the rotting original to instal, at least, a reminder of its design? The first impulse of those who are not architects is to keep, ever so little longer, what they can of the very substance itself at all costs to the future. But let us reflect a little. Those designers of the Middle Ages who were concerned with that original cared nothing for the individual stone or stick—would not even have cared for it had it acquired the history that it now possesses; their minds were centered on the aforesaid form, with, possibly, its colour and endurance, all which qualities it is now rapidly losing. Why then should we prize what they neglected, and neglect what they prized?

This is rather a large question for the end of a lecture. Out of it arises a conflict between the purely æsthetic sense and the memorial or associative. The artist instinct and the caretaking instinct part company over the disappearing creation. The true architect, who is first of all an artist and not an antiquary, is naturally most influenced by the æsthetic sense, his desire being, like Nature's, to retain, recover, or re-create the idea which has become damaged, without much concern about the associations of the material that idea may have been displayed in. Few occupations are more pleasant than that of endeavouring to re-capture an old design from the elusive hand of annihilation.

Thus if the architect have also an antiquarian bias he is pulled in two directions—in one by his wish to hand on or modify the abstract form, in the other by his reverence for the antiquity of its embodiment.

Architects have been much blamed for their doings in respect of old churches, and no doubt they have much to answer for. Yet one cannot logically blame an archi-

Life and Art

tect for being an architect—a chief craftsman, constructor, creator of forms—not their preserver.

If I were practising in that profession I would not, I think, undertake a church restoration in any circumstances. I should reply, if asked to do so, that a retired tinker or riveter of old china, or some 'Old Mortality' from the almshouse, would superintend the business better. In short, the opposing tendencies excited in an architect by the distracting situation can find no satisfactory reconciliation.

Fortunately cases of imminent disappearance are not the most numerous of those on which the Society has to pronounce an opinion. The bulk of the work of preservation lies in organising resistance to the enthusiasm for newness in those parishes, priests, and churchwardens who regard a church as a sort of villa to be made convenient and fashionable for the occupiers of the moment; who say, 'Give me a wide chancel arch—they are "in" at present'; who pull down the west gallery to show the new west window, and pull out old irregular pews to fix mathematically spaced benches for a congregation that never comes.

Those who are sufficiently in touch with these proceedings may be able to formulate some practical and comprehensive rules for the salvation of such few—very few —old churches, diminishing in number every day, as chance to be left intact owing to the heathen apathy of their parson and parishioners in the last century. The happy accident of indifferentism in those worthies has preserved their churches to be a rarity and a delight to pilgrims of the present day. The policy of 'masterly inaction'—often the greatest of all policies—was never practised to higher gain than by these, who simply left their historic buildings alone. To do nothing, where to act on little knowledge is a dangerous thing, is to do most and best.

Dialect in Novels

First appeared in *The Athenaeum,* November 30, 1878. Reprinted in John Lane's *Bibliography;* included in Johnson's *Art of Thomas Hardy,* edition of 1923.

A SOMEWHAT vexed question is re-opened in your criticism of my story, 'The Return of the Native'; namely, the representation in writing of the speech of the peasantry, when that writing is intended to show mainly the character of the speakers, and only to give a general idea of their linguistic peculiarities.

An author may be said to fairly convey the spirit of intelligent peasant talk if he retains the idiom, compass, and characteristic expressions, although he may not encumber the page with obsolete pronunciations of the purely English words, and with mispronunciations of those derived from Latin and Greek. In the printing of standard speech, hardly any phonetic principle at all is observed; and if a writer attempts to exhibit on paper the precise accents of a rustic speaker, he disturbs the proper balance of a true representation by unduly insisting upon the grotesque element; thus directing attention to a point of inferior interest and diverting it from the speaker's meaning, which is by far the chief concern where the aim is to depict the men and their natures rather than their dialect forms.

On the Use of Dialect

First appeared in *The Spectator*, October 15, 1881.

[To the Editor of the 'Spectator.']

SIR,—In your last week's article on the 'Papers of the Manchester Literary Club,' there seems a slight error, which, though possibly accidental, calls for a word of correction from myself. In treating of dialect in novels, I am instanced by the writer as one of two popular novelists 'whose thorough knowledge of the dialectical peculiarities of certain districts has tempted them to write whole conversations which are, to the ordinary reader, nothing but a series of linguistic puzzles.' So much has my practice been the reverse of this (as a glance at my novels will show), that I have been reproved for too freely translating dialect-English into readable English, by those of your contemporaries who attach more importance to the publication of local nice-ties of speech than I do. The rule of scrupulously pre-serving the local idiom, together with the words which have no synonym among those in general use, while print-ing in the ordinary way most of those local expressions which are but a modified articulation of words in use elsewhere, is the rule I usually follow; and it is, I believe, generally recognised as the best, where every such rule must of necessity be a compromise, more or less unsatis-factory to lovers of form. It must, of course, be always a matter for regret that, in order to be understood,

On the Use of Dialect

writers should be obliged thus slightingly to treat varieties of English which are intrinsically as genuine, grammatical, and worthy of the royal title as is the all-prevailing competitor which bears it, whose only fault was that they happened not to be central, and therefore were worsted in the struggle for existence, when a uniform tongue became a necessity among the advanced classes of the population.—I am, Sir, &c.,

Why I Don't Write Plays

First appeared in *The Pall Mall Gazette,* August 31, 1892, and in *The Pall Mall Budget,* with facsimile and photograph, September 1, 1892. William Archer, writing in the *Fortnightly Review,* had urged the desirability of a reunion between literature and the drama, had suggested that living novelists were to blame for the divorce, and that they owed it to themselves to make some essay in dramatic form. Whereupon *The Pall Mall Gazette* invited the leading novelists to answer the following questions:
1. Whether you regard the present divorce of fiction from the drama as beneficial or inimical to the best interests of literature and the stage.
2. Whether you yourself have at any time had, or now have, any desire to exercise your gifts in the production of plays as well as of novels; and if not,
3. Why you consider the novel the better or more convenient means for bringing your ideas before the public you address.
Hardy's reply follows:

INIMICAL to the best interests of the stage: no injury to literature.

2. Have occasionally had a desire to produce a play, and have, in fact, written the skeletons of several. Have no such desire in any special sense just now.

3. Because, in general, the novel affords scope for getting nearer to the heart and meaning of things than does the play: in particular the play as nowadays conditioned, when parts have to be moulded to actors, not

[116]

Why I Don't Write Plays

actors to parts; when managers will not risk a truly original play; when scenes have to be arranged in a constrained and arbitrary fashion to suit the exigencies of scene-building, although spectators are absolutely indifferent to order and succession, provided they can have set before them a developing thread of interest. The reason of this arbitrary arrangement would seem to be that the presentation of human passions is subordinated to the presentation of mountains, cities, clothes, furniture, plate, jewels and other real and sham-real appurtenances, to the neglect of the principle that the material stage should be a conventional or figurative arena, in which accessories are kept down to the plane of mere suggestions of place and time so as not to interfere with the high-relief of the action and emotions.

On the Tree of Knowledge

First appeared in *The New Review*, May, 1894.
It was Hardy's contribution to a symposium of
opinions on the physiological aspects of marriage, questions of sexual morality, etc. Other
contributors included Hall Caine, Walter Besant, Björnsen, Zangwill.

TO your first inquiry I would answer that a girl
should certainly not be allowed to enter into
matrimony without a full knowledge of her probable future in that holy estate, and of the possibilities
which may lie in the past of the elect man.

I have not much faith in an innocent girl's 'discovery
of the great mysteries of life' by means of 'the ordinary
intercourse of society.' Incomplete presentations, vi-
cious presentations, meretricious and seductive presentations, are not unlikely in pursuing such investigations
through such a channel.

What would seem to be the most natural course is the
answer to your second question: that a plain handbook
on natural processes, specially prepared, should be
placed in the daughter's hands, and, later on, similar information on morbid contingencies. Innocent youths
should, I think, also receive the same instruction; for (if
I may say a word out of my part) it has never struck me
that the spider is invariably male and the fly invariably
female.

As your problems are given on the old lines so I take
them, without entering into the general question whether

On the Tree of Knowledge

marriage, as we at present understand it, is such a desirable goal for all women as it is assumed to be; or whether civilisation can escape the humiliating indictment that, while it has been able to cover itself with glory in the arts, in literatures, in religions, and in the sciences, it has never succeeded in creating that homely thing, a satisfactory scheme for the conjunction of the sexes.

Laws the Cause of Misery

First appeared in *Hearst's Magazine*, June, 1912, with portrait. It was Hardy's contribution to a symposium of answers to the question, 'How Shall We Solve the Divorce Problem?' Other contributors included William Howard Taft, William De Morgan, Hall Caine, Winston Churchill, Theodore Dreiser, Ernest Shackleton.

I HAVE already said many times, during the past twenty or thirty years, that I regard Marriage as a union whose terms should be regulated entirely for the happiness of the community, including, primarily, that of the parties themselves.

As the English marriage laws are, to the eyes of anybody who looks around, the gratuitous cause of at least half the misery of the community, that they are allowed to remain in force for a day is, to quote the famous last word of the ceremony itself, an 'amazement,' and can only be accounted for by the assumption that we live in a barbaric age, and are the slaves of gross superstition.

As to what should be done, in the unlikely event of any amendment of the law being tolerated by bigots, it is rather a question for experts than for me. I can only suppose, in a general way, that a marriage should be dissolvable at the wish of either party, if that party prove it to be a cruelty to him or her, provided (probably) that the maintenance of the children, if any, should be borne by the breadwinner.

Appreciation of Anatole France

First appeared in *The Times*, London, December 11, 1913. On December 10, 1913, a banquet in honor of M. France was held at the Savoy. Hardy, unable to be present, sent this message to the Chairman, Lord Redesdale, who read it and gave it out for publication. The MS. was in the possession of M. France until his death.

I PARTICULARLY regret that, though one of the Committee, I am unable to be present to meet M. Anatole France at the reception on Wednesday. In these days when the literature of narrative and verse seems to be losing its qualities as an art, and to be assuming a structureless, conglomerate character, it is a privilege that we should have come into our midst a writer who is faithful to the principles that make for permanence, who never forgets the value of organic form and symmetry, the force of reserve, and the emphasis of understatement, even in his lighter works.

The War and Literature

First appeared in *The Book Monthly,* April, 1915. An answer to the banal question, popular at the time, 'What effect is the War likely to exert over literary production?'

ULTIMATELY for good; by 'removing (from literature) those things that are shaken, as things that are made, that those things that cannot be shaken may remain.'—Heb. xii. 27.

To Tinsley

First appeared in *The Atlantic Monthly*, March, 1915, in A. Edward Newton's article, *Amenities of Book Collecting*. Mr. Newton acquired the manuscript from a bookseller for five shillings.

BOCKHAMPTON,
DORCHESTER, Dec. 20, 1870.

SIR:—I believe I am right in understanding your terms thus—that if the gross receipts reach the costs of publishing I shall receive the £75 back again, and if they are more than the costs I shall have £75, added to half the receipts beyond the costs (*i.e.*, assuming the expenditure to be £100 the receipt £200 I should have returned to me £75 + 50 = 125). Will you be good enough to say too if the sum includes advertising to the customary extent, and about how long after my paying the money the book would appear?

Yours faithfully,

THOMAS HARDY.

On the Treatment of a Certain Author

First appeared in *The Athenaeum,* November 22, 1890. It is an interesting comment on a curious controversy involving William Black and Rudyard Kipling, from whom it drew the sharp verses of 'The Rhyme of the Three Captains.'

NOVEMBER 17, 1890.

OUR attention has been called—somewhat late, perhaps—to a passage in the 'Literary Gossip' of the *Athenaeum* of October 4th, in which the case of a certain author against Messrs. Harper & Brothers is first mentioned. It is no part of our purpose to express an opinion upon this case. But it seems a clear duty to us, who have experienced honourable treatment from this firm, to enter a protest against the sweeping condemnation passed upon them in the paragraph in question. This paragraph does not take the form of a communication by a contributor singly responsible for his own opinion, but it carries the whole weight and authority of the greatest literary journal in the country. 'When,' says this editorial note, 'an author is unknown to fame, they, it would seem, content themselves with insulting him; when he is celebrated, they insult and rob him.'

We wish to record the fact that in the course of many years' friendly business relations with Messrs. Harper & Brothers such has not been our experience. Whenever it is a question of acquiring for any of their periodicals the

[126]

On the Treatment of a Certain Author

foreign author's rights, they are as just and liberal in their dealings as any English house. In the matter of book publication we have always found them willing and desirous to do what is possible for the foreign author, whose interests the American law not only fails to protect, but entirely ignores.

WALTER BESANT.
WILLIAM BLACK.
THOMAS HARDY.

On Censorship of the Drama

First appeared in *The Academy*, August 14, 1909.

SOMETHING or other—which probably is consciousness of the Censor—appears to deter men of letters, who have other channels for communicating to the public, from writing for the stage. As an ounce of experience is worth a ton of theory, I may add the ballad which I published in the *English Review* for last December, entitled 'A Sunday Morning Tragedy,' I wished to produce as a tragic play before I printed the ballad form of it, and I went so far as to shape the scenes, action, etc.; but it then occurred to me that the subject—one in which the fear of transgressing convention overrules natural feeling to the extent of bringing dire disaster—the eminently proper and moral subject, would prevent my getting it on the boards, so I abandoned it.

THOMAS HARDY.

On 'Tess' in America

First appeared in *The Critic*, September, 1892.

MAX GATE, DORCHESTER, Aug. 26th, 1892.

TO THE EDITORS OF THE CRITIC:—
A complaint has reached me from your pages to the effect that even in the revised and enlarged American edition of 'Tess of the D'Urbervilles' I have thought fit to suppress the explanatory preface which appears in all the English editions.

I find it to be quite true that the preface is omitted; but you will perhaps allow me to assure your readers that such omission was not intentional on my part, but arose from circumstances of publication over which I had no control at the time.

I am now taking measures to attach to the American edition both the original preface and a new preface which is in preparation for the fifth English edition.

I may add in this connection that the necessity for (at least) simultaneous publication in America of English books, to secure copyright, renders it almost impossible that the latest addenda of an author should be incorporated in the foreign imprint. Could even a fortnight's grace be allowed, final touches, given just before going to press on this side, would not be excluded from American copies as they now are in so many cases.

Yours faithfully,

THOMAS HARDY.

[129]

On Recognition of Authors by the State

First appeared in *The Bookman* (London),
December, 1891.

SIR,—I daresay it would be very interesting that literature should be honoured by the State. But I don't see how it could be satisfactorily done. The highest flights of the pen are often, indeed mostly, the excursions and revelations of souls unreconciled to life; while the natural tendency of a government would be to encourage acquiescence in life as it is. However, I have not thought much about the matter.

THOMAS HARDY.

Maeterlinck's Apology for Nature

First appeared in *The Academy*, May 17, 1902.
It was a comment on the review of the essay,
The Mystery of Justice, in Maeterlinck's 'The
Buried Temple,' translated by Alfred Sutro,
which had appeared in *The Academy* of May 3,
1902. The letter is reprinted in Brennecke's
'Thomas Hardy's Universe.'

SIR,—In your review of M. Maeterlinck's book you quote with seeming approval his vindication of Nature's ways, which is (as I understand it) to the effect that, though she does not appear to be just from our point of view, she may practice a scheme of morality unknown to us, in which she is just. Now, admit but the bare possibility of such a hidden morality, and she would go out of court without the slightest stain on her character, so certain should we feel that indifference to morality was beneath her greatness.

Far be it from my wish to disturb any comforting fantasy, if it be barely tenable. But alas, no profound reflection can be needed to detect the sophistry in M. Maeterlinck's argument, and to see that the original difficulty recognised by thinkers like Schopenhauer, Hartmann, Haeckel, &c., and by most of the persons called pessimists, remains unsurmounted.

Pain has been, and pain is: no new sort of morals in Nature can remove pain from the past and make it pleasure for those who are its infallible estimators, the bearers thereof. And no injustice, however slight, can be atoned for by her future generosity, however ample,

Life and Art

so long as we consider Nature to be, or to stand for, unlimited power. The exoneration of an omnipotent Mother by her retrospective justice becomes an absurdity when we ask, What made the foregone injustice necessary to Her Omnipotence?

So you cannot, I fear, save her good name except by assuming one of two things: that she is blind, and not a judge of her actions, or that she is an automaton, and unable to control them; in either of which assumptions, though you have the chivalrous satisfaction of screening one of her sex, you only throw responsibility a stage further back.

But the story is not new. It is true, nevertheless, that, as M. Maeterlinck contends, to dwell too long amid such reflections does no good, and that to model our conduct on Nature's apparent conduct, as Nietzsche would have taught, can only bring disaster to humanity. —Yours truly,

THOMAS HARDY.

Max Gate, Dorchester.

On 'The Well-Beloved'

First appeared in *The Academy*, March 27, 1897.

DORCHESTER: March 29.

AFTER reading your review of 'The Well-Beloved' (more appreciative in feeling and generous towards its faults than such a slight story deserves), I think it would not be amiss to account for the ultra-romantic notion of the tale, which seems to come slightly as a surprise to readers. Not only was it published serially five years ago, but it was sketched many years before that date when I was comparatively a young man and interested in the Platonic Idea, which, considering its charm and its poetry, one could well wish to be interested in always.

Later on, in answer to a request from Mr. Tillotson, of Bolton, for 'something light' for his syndicate, the tale was taken in hand and adapted, the idea of perfection in woman being made to grow upon the hero, an innocent and moral man throughout, as described, till it became a trouble to him rather than a delight.

In lately correcting and revising the chapters I saw that the visionary character of the conception, and, so to speak, the youthfulness of the plot, was what I should certainly not have been able to enter into at this time of my life, if it had not been shaped already. There is, of course, underlying the fantasy followed by the

[133]

Life and Art

visionary artist the truth that all men are pursuing a shadow, the Unattainable, and I venture to hope that this may redeem the tragi-comedy from the charge of frivolity, or of being built upon a baseless conceit, that may otherwise have been brought against it.

I may, perhaps, be allowed to state in addition, that 'Avice' is an old name common in the county, and that 'Caro' (like all the other surnames) is an imitation of a local name which will occur to everybody who knows the place—this particular modification having been adopted because of its resemblance to the Italian for 'dear.'

THOMAS HARDY.

To Clement K. Shorter

First appeared in *The Academy*, September 7, 1901, as a reply to some tourists' slighting remarks about the Dorset country.

THIS statement is rather unfair to Wessex, and, indeed, quite inaccurate, as will be evident when it is explained that the party of visitors did not go near the 'intrinsically romantic' spots imperfectly described in the novels, but, like almost all tourists, adhered for the most part to the London highway and the branch highway passing through the heath district, which is rather impressive and lonely than 'romantic' or 'beautiful.' Had they, for instance, visited Shaston or Shaftesbury, Bullbarrow, Nettlecombe Tout, Dogberry Hill, High Stoy, Cross in Hand, Bubb Down Hill, Toller Down, Wynyard's Gap, and a dozen other such places for inland scenery, and the coast cliffs between Swanage and Lyme Regis for marine, such a remark could not have been made. But then, most of these spots lie miles out of the regular way, and few of them can be reached except on foot. The pilgrims were not absent from London much more than twelve hours altogether, returning there the same evening; and it is utterly impossible to see the recesses of this county in such a manner, not to mention those adjoining.

THOMAS HARDY.

[135]

On the War

(a) First appeared in *The Times,* London, October 7, 1914.
(b) First appeared in *The Manchester Guardian,* October 12, 1914.

(a)

EVERYBODY is able to feel in a general way the loss to the world that has resulted from this mutilation of a noble building, which was almost the finest specimen of mediæval architecture in France. The late M. Viollet-le-Duc, who probably knew more about French architecture than any man of his time, considered it to unite in itself in a unique degree the charms of beauty and dignity. But the majority of people have found comfort in a second thought—that the demolished parts can be renewed, even if not without vast expense. Only those who for professional or other reasons have studied in close detail the architecture of the thirteenth and fourteenth centuries are aware that to do this in its entirety is impossible. Gothic architecture has been a dead art for the last three hundred years, in spite of the imitations thrown broadcast over the land, and much of what is gone from the fine structure is gone for ever.

The magnificent stained glass of the cathedral will probably be found to have suffered the most. How is that to be renewed? Some of it dated from the thirteenth century, and is inimitable by any handiworkers

[136]

On the War

in the craft nowadays. Its wreck is all the more to be regretted in that, if I remember rightly, many of the windows had already in the past lost their original glass. Then the sculpture and the mouldings, and other details. Moreover, their antique history was a part of them, and how can that history be imparted to a renewal? When I was young French architecture of the best period was much investigated, and selections from such traceries and mouldings as those at Rheims were delineated with the greatest accuracy and copied by architects' pupils—myself among the rest. It seems strange indeed now that the curves we used to draw with such care should have been broken as ruthlessly as if they were a cast-iron railing replaceable from a mould. If I had been told three months ago that any inhabitants of Europe would wilfully damage such a masterpiece as Rheims in any circumstances whatever, I should have thought it an incredible statement.

Is there any remote chance of the devastation being accidental, or partly accidental, or contrary to the orders of a superior officer? This ought to be irrefutably established and settled, since upon it depends the question whether German civilisation shall become a byword for ever or no. Should it turn out to be a predetermined destruction—as an object-lesson of the German ruling caste's will to power—it will strongly suggest that a disastrous blight upon the glory and nobility of that great nation has been wrought by the writings of Nietzsche, with his followers, Treitschke, Bernhardi, &c. I should think there is no instance since history began of a country being so demoralised by a single writer, the irony being that he was a megalomaniac and not

Life and Art

truly a philosopher at all. What puzzles one is to understand how the profounder thinkers of Germany, and to some extent, elsewhere, can have been so dazzled by this writer's bombastic poetry—for it is a sort of prose-poetry—as to be blinded to the fallacy of his arguments—if they can be called arguments which are off-hand assumptions. His postulates as to what life is on this earth have no resemblance to reality. Yet he and his school seem to have eclipsed for the time in Germany the close-reasoned philosophers—such men as Kant and Schopenhauer. It is rather rough on the latter that their views of life should be swept into one net with those of Nietzsche, Treitschke, and the rest as 'German philosophy' (as has been done by some English writers to the papers) when they really differ further in ethics than the humane philosophers mentioned differ in that respect from Christianity.

(b)

To the Editor of the Manchester Guardian.

Sir,—I would gladly, if at this stage of my life I could reopen what is an old subject with me, reply to your correspondents who think I have misrepresented Nietzsche (at the fag-end of a letter on an architectural subject, by the way). I will only remark that I have never said he was a German, or that he loved Germany, or that he lived before Treitschke; or that he did not express such sentiments as your correspondents and others—apparently young men chiefly—quote to the avoidance of other sentiments that I could quote, *e.g.:*

On the War

Ye shall love peace as a means to new wars, and the short peace better than the long. . . . I do not counsel you to conclude peace but to conquer. . . . Beware of pity.

He used to seem to me (I have not looked into his works for years) to be an incoherent rhapsodist who jumps from Machiavelli to Isaiah as the mood seizes him, and whom it is impossible to take seriously as a mentor. I may have been wrong, but he impressed me in the long run, owing to the preternatural absence of any overt sign of levity in him, with a curious suspicion (no doubt groundless) of his being a first-class Swiftian humourist in disguise.

I need hardly add that with many of his sayings I have always heartily agreed; but I feel that few men who have lived long enough to see the real colour of life, and who have suffered, can believe in Nietzsche as a thinker.—Yours, &c.

THOMAS HARDY.

To the Stevenson Club

First appeared in *The Times*, London, August, 1923.

I MUCH appreciate the suggestion of the Committee of the London R. L. Stevenson Club that I should become an honorary member, even though, as a matter of fact, I am not what would be called a Stevensonian, in the full sense in which that expression could be applied to so many, probably all, of the club's members. However, the question of my sufficiency does not really arise. I have now reached a great age: one at which I find it necessary to abstain from further association with societies, even if only of an honorary kind, flattering as the connexion may be, and, therefore, I must decline the distinction of being elected one of the London branch of the club.

THOMAS HARDY.